Complete
Knitting

Complete Knitting

Techniques & Projects

CREATIVE HOMEOWNER® Home Arts

First Published in North America in 2006 by

CRE🏠TIVE
HOMEOWNER®

Creative Homeowner® is a registered trademark of
Federal Marketing Corporation

ISBN 10: 1-58011-291-9
ISBN 13: 978-1-58011-291-8
Library of Congress Catalog Card Number: 2006929856

Current printing (last digit)
10 9 8 7 6 5 4 3 2 1

Produced by Collins & Brown
151 Freston Road
London
W10 6TH

An imprint of Anova Books Company Ltd

Commissioning Editor: Michelle Lo
Design Manager: Gemma Wilson
Editor: Marie Clayton
Photographer: Mark Winwood
Knitwear Designers: Kate Buchanan, Louise Butt,
Laura Long, Sîan Luyken.
Designer: Ben Kracknell Studios
Production Controller: Laura Brodie
Editorial Assistant: Katie Hudson

Printed and bound in China

CREATIVE HOMEOWNER
A Division of Federal Marketing Corp.
24 Park Way
Upper Saddle River, NJ 07458

www.creativehomeowner.com

Contents

Introduction

The craft of knitting has been enjoying a huge new popularity in recent years. From being something with a rather old-fashioned reputation that only older people knew how to do, it has become fun and trendy and an absorbing pastime for young and old alike. The basics are really simple—you just need to know how to cast on, knit and purl, and how to bind off at the end. This will give you the basics to create any stitch pattern, and with the addition of other simple shaping skills to add and decrease stitches, a couple of decorative techniques—and a bit of practice—you will soon be able to knit almost anything.

The other great thing about knitting is that it is really portable. Unlike some other crafts, it does not require space, lots of special tools or access to water or electricity. You really can knit almost anywhere—at home, on the beach, waiting in a line! Most large projects are made up of smaller units, so you can carry your knitting around to do whenever you have a spare minute. If you do have to leave it for some time, it will still be there, in the same condition, waiting to be picked up and completed. It's the ideal craft for a busy person—you can devote as much or as little time as you choose.

Hand-knitted garments are not necessarily cheaper than store-bought ones—that is not the point. The joy of creating your own item is that it really can be unique to you. The designer creates the pattern, but even if you follow it exactly you can still choose a different color yarn and make something that does not look exactly like the same item knitted by someone else. When you have a little skill and confidence you can customize even more—substitute a different edging, for instance, or change the fringe for a row of pompoms or a lacy trim.

At the back of this book you will find 25 diverse and exciting projects by designers Kate Buchanan, Louise Butt, Laura Long and Sîan Luyken to get you started. They include accessories, clothes, projects for the home and items for babies and children, and are suitable for a range of skill levels. Expand your wardrobe with the simple Drop-Stitch Cardigan or the Blue Note Hat and Scarf; make the Loopee Rug or the Lace Cushion to decorate your home.

Knitting is great fun, it's versatile and it's also addictive! Pick up your needles and yarn, grab this book, and off you go.

Getting Started

Just a few inexpensive pieces of equipment
are required for knitting. You may already
have most of these, and needles can be acquired
gradually as the need for them arises.

Equipment

When you first begin knitting you only need a few essential pieces of equipment, such as needles, tape measure, scissors, pins, and a yarn needle. There are several other items that may make your life easier—such as stitch holders, circular needles, and split ring markers—but they can be collected as and when you need them.

Needles—Pairs of needles are available in a range of materials including metal, plastic, wood and bamboo. Whatever material they are made of, needles are sized using a standard system—but there are three different systems, all of which are widely recognized, so one or more will be quoted in most knitting patterns. The US has its own system, Europe and the UK use a metric system, and there are also still needles sized using an old UK and Canadian system (see the conversion table to the right for the most common sizes). As well as varying sizes, needles come in different lengths to accommodate different numbers of stitches. There are also some special kinds for specific applications:

Stitch holders—resemble large safety pins and are used to hold stitches that will be worked on later. You could use a length of yarn threaded through the stitches and knotted instead. For just a few stitches, a large safety pin will do.

Cable needles—are short, double-pointed needles used when moving groups of stitches in cable or twisted stitch patterns. They come in a smaller range of sizes than ordinary needles and those with a kink or bend are easier to use.

Circular and double-pointed needles—designed mainly for knitting tubular or circular fabrics. Circular

Needle Conversion Chart

U.S. size	Metric	Old UK/Canadian size
0	2.00 mm	14
1	2.25 mm	13
–	2.50 mm	–
2	2.75 mm	12
–	3.00 mm	11
3	3.25 mm	10
4	3.50 mm	–
5	3.75 mm	9
6	4.00 mm	8
7	4.50 mm	7
8	5.00 mm	6
9	5.50 mm	5
10	6.00 mm	4
10½	6.50 mm	3
–	7.00 mm	2
–	7.50 mm	1
11	8.00 mm	0
13	9.00 mm	00
15	10.00 mm	000

needles are also sometimes used for flat knitting with a large number of stitches, since they can hold a great many stitches comfortably with the weight of the work evenly balanced between two hands. For small tubular items, such as socks or gloves, a set of four or more double pointed needles is usually used.

Tape measure—used to measure the gauge square and also the dimensions of the knitted fabric as you work. Fabric tapes can stretch with age, making measurements inaccurate, so check regularly and buy a new one if necessary.

Scissors—a small, sharp pair of scissors are useful to snip yarn.

Dressmaker's pins—these are used to hold pieces of knitting together for sewing, for marking off stitches and rows in a gauge swatch and for pinning pieces out for blocking or pressing. Choose long pins with colored heads.

Row counter—this is a small cylindrical device with a dial used to record the number of rows when this is critical, as when increasing or decreasing. It is slipped onto one needle before starting to knit and pushed up to the end. You must remember to turn the dial at the end of each row.

Split ring markers—these are little clips that can be attached to knitting to mark the beginning of a round in circular knitting, or for marking points in a stitch pattern.

Safety pins—a selection of large safety pins are useful to hold small numbers of stitches, as markers instead of the split ring, and to roughly hold pieces together to check dimensions before sewing up.

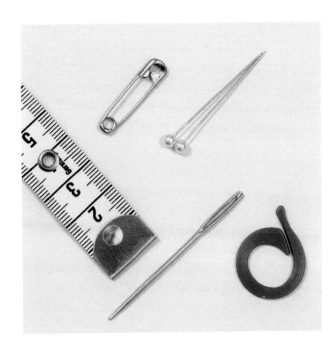

Tapestry or yarn needle—this type of needle has a blunt point so it will not split or snag the yarn. It is used for sewing seams and needs to have an eye large enough to thread the yarn.

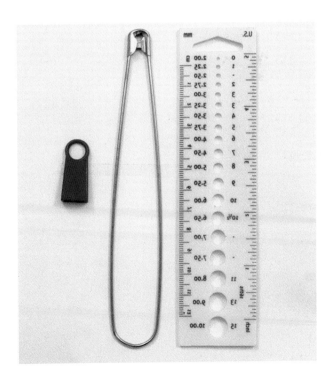

Fastenings

It is a good idea to consider the fastenings you may need for your garment at the same time as you buy the yarn. Most yarn stores also carry a range of fastenings and it will be quicker and easier to match the color of buttons or zippers to your yarn at the same time, rather than having to search for the right thing later.

Buttons—these are made in many materials, including plastic, ceramic, glass and wood. Make sure they are washable if the garment is to be washable, otherwise you will have to remove the buttons each time you clean the item. Consider the style of the garment when choosing the buttons—small, delicate pearl ones look best on a lacy garment, while big chunky ones usually work best on a thick outdoor garment.

Zipper—if you cannot get a zipper in the exact shade to match your yarn, choose one a little darker rather than lighter. If you have the zipper before you start knitting you can adjust the length of the garment to match it, if necessary.

Hook and eyes—these are usually used as a concealed fastening and come in a very wide range of sizes. They are useful on their own as a top fastening at the collar or on a waistband, but are usually combined with buttons or a zipper for a long opening.

Snaps—also an invisible fastening, but they will not hold under a heavy strain. They are useful on garments for young children, as they may find snaps easier to fasten than buttons.

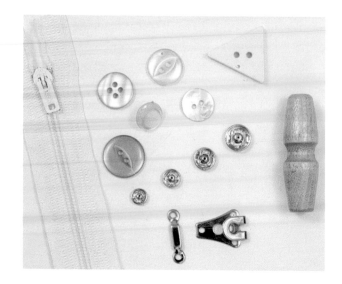

Fasten Nation

Fastenings can make a big difference to how your finished garment will look, so spend some time getting the right thing. Cheap buttons may make your lovely handmade garment look mass-produced.

Remember that buttons and zippers do not have to tone in with the knitted fabric—on the right project you can choose something in a contrasting color to make the fastenings into a feature. See Kate Buchanan's Mable Cable Hat on page 144 for a creative use of buttons!

Unusual fastenings can often be found in specialist stores, antique shops or thrift stores. If you see something unusual or particularly beautiful, buy it even if you don't have an immediate use for it—keep it in your stash for a future project.

After making the first buttonhole, check the fit on your chosen button before you continue to make the others. If it is too small you can either try remaking the buttonhole in a larger size or choose smaller buttons. If it is too large, you can make it smaller next time.

Yarns

Yarn is the general term used for strands of fiber that are twisted together into a continuous thread. It covers both natural fibers, such as wool, cotton and silk, and synthetic ones, such as nylon, viscose, or acrylic. It also covers varying thicknesses and both smooth and textured finishes. Synthetic yarns are strong, hardwearing, and easy to wash, but they often lack some of the fine qualities of natural yarns.

Most yarns are categorized according to the number or strands, or plies, they are made up of and by weight. Generally, the lower the ply, the thinner the yarn and the lighter the final garment will be. However, yarns in the same ply are not necessarily identical and each also comes in a range of materials. If pure wool yarn is too scratchy next to the skin, try cotton or a wool/cotton mix. As well as smooth, traditional yarns there are now also lots of unusual novelty yarns such as the furry yarn used in the Foxy Cushion on page 122.

Fingering or 4-ply
This lightweight yarn works well for lacy garments and is available in an excellent wide range of colors and finishes.

Sport or Double Knitting (DK)
This is one of the most popular of the standard yarns and is suitable for most garments.

Aran
This yarn was traditionally cream in color and used for classic Aran designs, but is now available in a range of shades.

Bulky or Chunky
This yarn is thicker than Aran and knits up very quickly. It is often used for making loose-fitting outdoor garments.

Choosing yarn
When learning to knit it is especially important to choose a yarn that feels comfortable in your hands—one that is slightly elastic and neither slippery nor so highly textured that it will not move smoothly through your fingers. Patterns normally specify exactly which brand of yarn to be used for a project. You can often substitute a different yarn for the one specified, providing that you can obtain the same gauge (see page 29). Try to use yarn with the same content as the one specified, if possible. Also check the length of yarn in the ball, as different types and brands have differing lengths—the length will be given on the ball band. If the length in the ball varies

significantly from that of the specified yarn, you may need more or less balls to complete the item. Always buy an extra ball of yarn anyway—if you do need a bit more later the same dye lot may not be available, but you can always use up extra yarn in another small project.

Ball band

The ball band gives much useful information about the yarn, including the content—for example, it may say 100% wool or 80% wool/20% angora—and washing and pressing instructions. It also gives the length within the ball, which is useful when substituting a different yarn; a 1¾oz/50g ball of pure cotton will contain less yarn than the same weight ball of pure wool, for instance.

Yarn labeling

Yarn is usually sold in balls or skeins. The company normally brands its yarn with a ball band or label that contains invaluable information about the yarn. Always keep the ball bands for reference purposes—dye lots, quantities, care instructions and so on.

Fiber Counts

After you have finished your item, keep the remains of the last ball of yarn with the ball band, so you will have both a reference for washing and care and spare yarn for later repairs.

Smooth yarns show up the detail of pattern stitches nicely, but textured or furry yarns can be more forgiving for the novice knitter.

Store spare yarn in clean plastic bags with a suitable natural moth repellent, such as cedar wood, wormwood rue, or tansy.

Needle sizes
Recommended knitting and crochet needlesize. You may need to use a different needle size, depending on your tension/gauge.

Tension/gauge square
Ideal tension/gauge of the yarn to achieve the best performance.

Shade
Usually represented by a number.

Dye lot
Batch number of the yarn.

Composition of the yarn

Weight and length

Brand name
Name of the company and of the yarn. Sometimes the company may also indicate the standard weight of the yarn, such as double knitting.

Washing instructions
Recommended aftercare advice.

SHADE 8308
LOT 348
100% COTTON
50g (85m)
BRAND NAME
Cotton DK
4 x 4in
24 st
30 rows
US 6
8UK
9UK F US
4mm

Patterns

*Each pattern gives a range of information at the beginning that will help
you knit the garment as its designer intended it to be.*

Equipment and yarn

This section gives the size of needles and any other
special equipment you will need to complete the
garment, although some basic tools, such as tape
measure, scissors, or pins will not be included. It also
gives the quantity of a specified yarn and any
fastenings or decorative bits that will be needed.

Sizing

Most patterns will give the size or sizes it is designed
for at the beginning, often with a set of actual
measurements as well. The actual measurements for
a particular size may vary quite a bit in patterns from
different designers or for different yarns, so it is
always worth checking them against a ready-made
garment with a good fit.

Gauge

The gauge required for the pattern will be expressed
in number of rows and stitches in a measured square,
when knitted in either stockinette stitch or the main
stitch used for the item. To produce an item as the
designer intended, you need to knit to the same
gauge. If not, the measurements will not come out
the same, so it is important that you make a swatch
to check your gauge before you begin. If you knit to a
different gauge you can change the size of needle you
use to adjust it—for instructions on how to make a
gauge swatch, see page 29.

Measurements Chart

Imperial (Inches)	Metric (Centimeters)
32–36	81–91.5
36–40	91.5–101.5
40–44	101.5–111.5

Abbreviations

Standard knitting abbreviations are given in this book
on page 169, but if the pattern has any special
instructions they will be written out in full at the
start, along with the abbreviation used in the pattern.

Pattern Repeats

Most stitch patterns, unless they are completely
random or worked in panels, are made up of a set
of stitches that are repeated across the row, and a
number of rows that are repeated throughout the
length of the fabric. A pattern repeat within knitting
instructions is contained within either brackets or
parentheses, or follows an asterisk (*). The extra
stitches outside the brackets or before the asterisk are
to balance the pattern within the piece of knitting.

Charts

Some patterns include a chart, particularly for color work. When you understand them, charts are very easy to follow because they give a reference of what the design should look like. Each block on the chart represents one stitch, and the design is shown by coding blocks to represent a color or stitch technique. The chart shows the design from the right side, so when you are working you read the even-numbered rows from left to right—exactly as you are knitting the stitches on the needle—and the odd-numbered ones from right to left. If the design is a repeating pattern usually only one repeat will be given in the chart, so you just carry on repeating it across the width of the fabric.

If the chart shows several alternative sizes of garment, it is advisable to mark the lines for the size you are following. Row numbers will be shown down one side of the chart—if the pattern is large or complicated you will need to use a row counter to keep track of where you are.

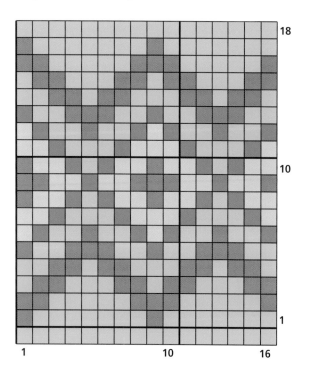

Adapting Patterns

When you become more confident you may want to adapt standard patterns, either to fit you better or to change elements of the design. Being able to change things to suit is one of the major advantages of knitting something yourself. Some things are easy to adapt—if you want slightly shorter sleeves or a slightly longer body you can just knit either a few less or a few more rows, as long as there is no shaping involved.

Always check the actual measurements of each part before you begin—you may find that the sleeves of one size are the right length, but the body of another size is a better length. There is nothing to stop you following the instructions for different sizes for different parts of a garment, but remember to go through the pattern before you begin, highlighting the size to follow at each stage.

If the pattern is for a plain garment but you want a motif, you can simply use the chart for the motif you want when you get to the position you wish to place it. Bear in mind that the motif may not come out exactly the same in different yarns. Alternatively, if you want to remove a motif, simply ignore the instructions for creating the motif. A plain garment can also be transformed by adding a decorative edging to hem and sleeves. In addition, you can also add texture or design by using a different stitch. See the Stitch Library on page 156 for more options.

Basic Techniques

Before casting on stitches you must get to grips with the needles and yarn.
At first, they will seem awkward to hold, but practice will soon make them familiar.
Use a medium-weight yarn and a pair of US 6 (4 mm) needles to practice with.

Holding the needles

There are several ways of holding the needles. The illustrations, shown here, demonstrate the English method, which gives a more even stitch. Sometimes left-handers may find the Continental method—in which most of the work is done by the left hand—easier to use. The Continental method does allow faster knitting, but it is much harder to obtain even stitches.

Holding the right needle

Hold the right needle in the same position as a pencil. For casting on and working the first few rows, the knitting passes between the thumb and index finger. As the knitting grows, slide your thumb under the knitted piece, holding the needle from below.

Holding the left needle

1 The left needle is held lightly, with the hand over the top. With the English method of knitting, the thumb and the index finger control the tip of the needle.

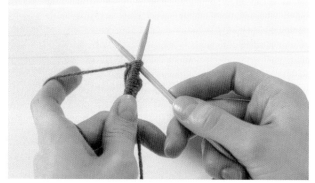

2 If you are using the Continental method of knitting, the tip of the needle is controlled with the thumb and middle finger and the yarn is held aloft with the index finger.

Holding the yarn

The yarn may either be held in the right hand, which is known as the English method, or in the left hand, which is the Continental method. Either way the working yarn must be wound round the fingers to control the tension on the yarn and produce even knitting. There are two main methods of doing this

Method 1
Holding the yarn in one hand, pass it under the little finger of the other hand, then around the same finger, over the third finger, under the center finger and over the index finger. The index finger is used to pass the yarn around the needle tip, and the yarn circled around the little finger creates an even, firm gauge.

Method 2
Holding the yarn in one hand, pass it under the little finger of the other hand, over the third finger, under the center finger and over the index finger. The index finger is used to pass the yarn around the needle tip, and the gauge is controlled by gripping the yarn in the crook of the little finger, which creates a looser gauge than Method 1.

Making a slip knot

A slip knot is the starting point for most casting on techniques. If the slip knot looks a bit loose compared to the other stitches, try casting on an extra stitch and then going back and pulling the slip knot out.

How to make a slip knot

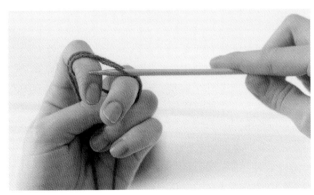

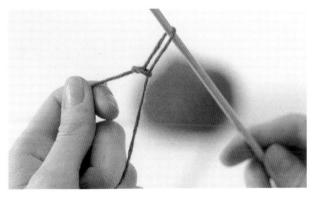

1 Wind the yarn twice around the first two fingers of the left hand as shown, then insert the tip of a knitting needle over the front loop and under the back one.

2 Pull the back loop through the front one and then pull on the two ends of yarn to tighten the loop on the needle.

Casting On

*This is the term used for making a row of stitches as a foundation
for knitting. Each casting on method produces a different type of edge, but the two
most common are the thumb method and the cable method. The thumb method
requires only one needle and is used for a very elastic edge or when the rows
immediately after the cast on stitches are worked in garter stitch (every row knitted).
The cable method requires two needles and gives a firm, neat finish.*

Thumb method

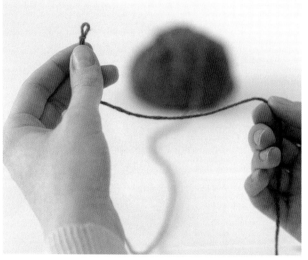

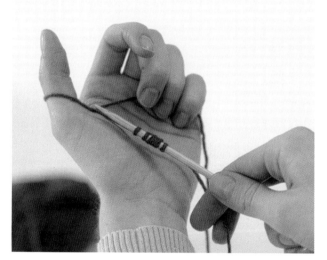

1 Measure an end of yarn about three times the finished width of the piece you are making, then make a slip knot and place on a needle.

2 Hold the needle in the right hand with the ball end of the yarn under the index finger, wind the cut end of the yarn round the thumb of the left hand from back to front.

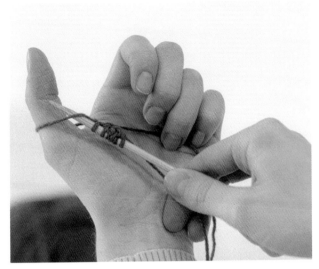

3 Insert the tip of the needle upwards through the loop of yarn on the thumb.

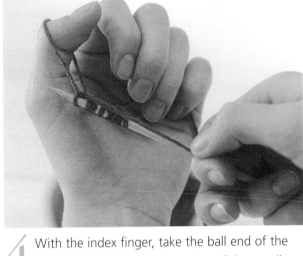

4 With the index finger, take the ball end of the yarn forward and over the point of the needle.

5 With the needle, pull the yarn back through the loop on the thumb to form a stitch. Remove the loop of yarn from the thumb and pull the loose end to tighten the stitch on the needle. Repeat steps 2–6 until you have cast on the number of stitches you need.

Thumbs up

The thumb method of casting on produces a very elastic edge, which is great for bands and borders in seed stitch (k1, p1 on each row to produce a dense textured fabric) or garter stitch (each row either knit or purl, see page 27).

Use the thumb method with yarns with only limited elasticity, such as pure cotton.

It is also the best technique to use when you are casting on for a straight garment with no pull in, such as a tunic, or if you are making a separate piece, such as a collar, pocket or an edging that is to be sewn on afterwards.

If you are casting on a great many stitches, mark every ten or so with a piece of contrasting yarn or a split ring stitch marker round the needle—this will make it faster to count up as you go or if you are interrupted.

Cable method

1 Make a slip knot near the cut end of the yarn and place it on the left needle.

2 Hold the yarn at the back of the needles. Insert the right needle upwards through the slip knot and with the index finger pass the yarn over the point of the needle.

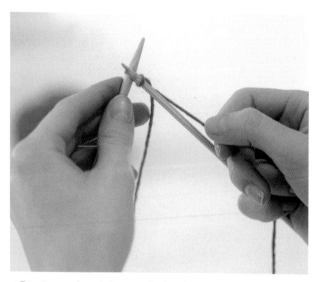

3 Draw the right needle back through the slip knot, pulling the yarn to form a loop on the right needle. Do not slip the original stitch off the left needle.

4 Insert the left needle from right to left through this loop and slip it off the right hand needle onto the left. There are now two stitches on the left needle.

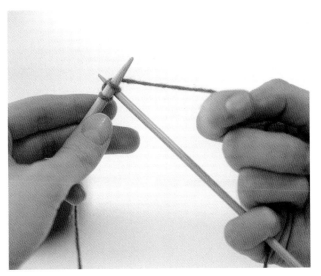

5 Insert the right needle between the two stitches on the left needle. Wind the yarn round the right needle.

6 Draw a loop through and place it on the left needle as before. Repeat steps 5–6 until you have cast on the number of stitches you need.

Cable Vision

The cable method produces a less elastic edge, so it is great for borders and bands that will pull in, such as ribbing (k1, p1 on first row, p1, k1 on alt row, see page 48). It is not so suitable if the border is to be in seed stitch or garter stitch.

The cable cast on is called this because it produces a line of overlapping stitches along the edge that looks like a cable—it has nothing to do with the cable technique of knitting.

Practice casting on until you can produce a neat and even edge—try producing a series of knitted squares in different colors to practice both casting on and getting the tension right on various stitches. These squares need not be wasted—they can be sewn together to make a patchwork afghan.

Basic Stitches

*There are two basic stitches in knitting: knit and purl. All stitch patterns
are based on one or both of these stitches, combined and/or varied in some way.
The knit stitch is the easier of the two. Practice this until you can work it smoothly,
then move on to the purl stitch. Note that these stitches are abbreviated "k"
and "p" in knitting patterns. Other abbreviations are listed on page 169.*

Knit stitch

1 Hold the needle with the cast on stitches in the
left hand. With the yarn at the back of the
work, insert the right needle through the front of the
first stitch on the left needle.

2 With the index finger of the right hand, wind
the yarn from left to right over the point of the
right needle.

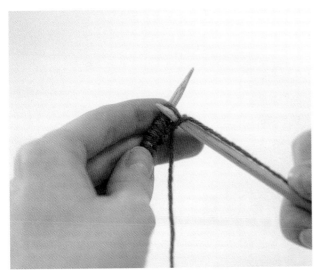

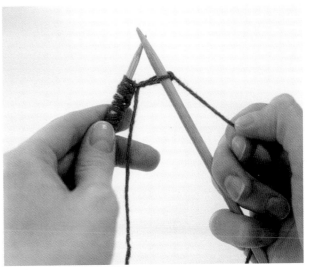

3 With the tip of the right needle, draw the yarn back through the stitch, forming a loop on the right needle.

4 Slip the original stitch off the left needle, keeping the new stitch on the right needle. Repeat steps 1–4 until all the stitches on the left hand needle have been worked and transferred to the right needle. You have now completed a knit row. Turn the work and transfer the needle with the stitches to the left hand, in preparation for working the next row.

5 If you work all knit rows, the result is called garter stitch and it looks like this.

Get Garter

Using garter stitch will make a completely reversible fabric, as both sides will have the same raised horizontal ridges.

Garter stitch produces a solid fabric that is thicker than stockinette stitch (see page 28) and does not curl, so it can be used on its own for bands and borders. It is particularly suitable for the bottom borders of straight garments that are not designed to pull in at the base.

Purl stitch

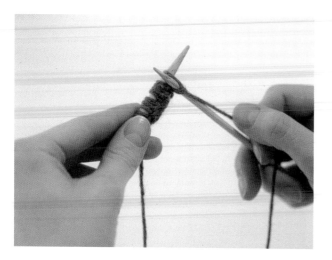

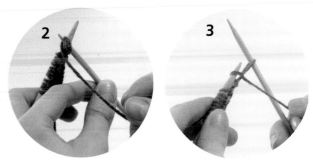

1 Hold the needle with the cast on stitches in the left hand. With the yarn at the front of the work, insert the right needle through the front of the first stitch on the left needle from back to front.

2 With the index finger of the right hand, wind the yarn from right to left over the point of the right needle.

3 With the tip of the right needle, draw the yarn back through the stitch, forming a loop on the right needle.

4 Slip the original stitch off the left needle, leaving the new stitch on the right needle. Repeat steps 1–4 until all the stitches on the left hand needle have been worked and transferred to the right needle. You have now completed a purl row. Turn the work and transfer the needle with the stitches to the left hand, in preparation for working the next row.

If you work one row knit, one row purl, the result is called stockinette stitch and it looks like this. The reverse side is sometimes used as the right side—it looks like a tighter version of garter stitch—in which case it is called reverse stockinette stitch. Stockinette stitch is abbreviated St st in patterns.

Working a Gauge Swatch

The gauge of a pattern is vitally important, because if you do not achieve the gauge stated, your garment will not come out to the right measurements. Even a very small difference in gauge can make a big difference across a whole garment, so it is important that you check your gauge before you start knitting. Using the yarn and needles given for the gauge in the pattern, work a square that is at least four stitches wider and four rows longer than needed for the correct gauge. The extra stitches and rows should mean that your gauge swatch will be bigger than stated in the pattern. Press the swatch and lay it flat, without stretching. Lay a ruler across horizontally and mark off 4 in. (10 cm) with two pins. Count the number of stitches between the pins. Lay the ruler vertically and mark off 4 in. (10 cm) with two pins. Count the number of rows between the pins. If you have more stitches and rows than given for the pattern gauge, try again with a size larger needles. If you have fewer stitches and rows than given for the pattern gauge, try again with a size smaller needles.

Making Fabrics

Congratulations! Now that you have learned the two
basic stitches, you have everything you need to
make a knitted fabric. Simply keep knitting rows, turn
the work as you get to the end and start again.
However, to join in new yarn, increase or decrease the
number of stitches on the needle, make buttonholes or to
finish your knitting off, you need a few more techniques.

Joining Yarn

Unless you are making something that only requires one ball of yarn, at some point you will have to join in a new ball. It is best to do this at the end of a row, so if you have less than four times the width of your knitting left in the old ball, join a new ball before you start the next row. The ends will need to be woven in, which can be done each time after you have worked a few more rows or all together when the whole piece is finished.

How to join a ball of yarn

To make a neat join, just drop the old yarn and start knitting with the new ball. To weave in the ends, thread a yarn needle with one end and take it under the loops of four or five stitches along the edge. Repeat with the other end in the opposite direction.

New Means to an End

If it is impossible to join in at the end of a row, just drop the old yarn just before you come to the end, leaving enough to sew the end in, and begin work with the new yarn—again leaving an end to sew in. After you have worked a few more rows you can sew in the ends.

Try to find time to sew in the ends as you go—otherwise you will have the boring job of sewing in all the ends in one go at the end before you can put everything together.

Decreasing

The easiest way of decreasing the number of stitches on the needle by one
stitch is to simply knit two stitches together. Decreasing the number of stitches in this way
is used for simple shaping, but also to create some stitch patterns.

Knitting two together on a knit row

Insert the right needle from left to right through two stitches instead of one, then knit them together as one stitch. This is called "knit two together" and the abbreviation in a pattern is k2tog.

Knitting two together on a purl row

Insert the right needle from right to left through two stitches instead of one, then purl them together as one stitch. This is called "purl two together" and the abbreviation in a pattern is p2tog.

Increasing

The easiest way of increasing the number of stitches on the needle by one stitch is to knit into the front and back of the same stitch, so making two stitches from one. This can be done on either a knit or a purl row. Another way is to make a stitch by working into the strand between the two stitches. Increasing the number of stitches is used both for simple shaping and to create some stitch patterns.

Working twice into one stitch on a knit row

Knit into the front of the stitch on the left needle in the normal way then, before slipping it off the needle, put the right needle behind the left one and knit again into the back of the same stitch. Slip the original stitch off the left needle.

Working twice into one stitch on a purl row

Purl into the front of the stitch on the left needle in the normal way then, before slipping it off the needle, put the right needle behind the left one and knit again into the back of the same stitch. Slip the original stitch off the left needle.

Make one

1 Insert the right needle from front to back under the horizontal strand that runs between the stitches on the needles.

2 Place the strand on the left needle, twisting it as shown to prevent a hole from forming. Knit or purl through the back of the loop.

3 Now you have a new stitch on the right needle, drop the strand from the left needle. Whether done with a knit or a purl stitch, this technique is called "make one" and the abbreviation in a patterns is m1.

More or Less...

Increasing and decreasing are not only used to shape pieces of knitting—they are also used in almost all lace patterns. Once you have mastered the technique and can increase and decrease easily, try out some of the lace patterns featured in the Stitch Workshop on pages 160–1.

Increases and decreases worked one or two stitches in from the edge give a neater edge, which is easier to pick up stitches along to add a knitted border—and also makes it easier to sew pieces together neatly. This technique is also called "fully fashioning" and is often used by designers as a decorative detail—see page 40 for more details of this technique.

The instructions in a pattern will tell you which technique to use, depending on which part of a garment you are working on.

Picking Up Stitches

If you need to add a decorative edge or a border to a piece of knitting, this can either be done by making it separately and sewing it on, or by picking up stitches along the edge and working on them to create the new edging. To pick up stitches evenly, divide the edge into equal spaces before you begin and work out how many stitches you need to pick up in each space to make up the total number required.

Picking up on a cast on or bound off edge

With right side facing, insert the point of the right needle from front to back under both loops of the cast on/bound off edge. Wind the yarn round the point of the needle and draw the loop through to create a new stitch. Continue until you have enough stitches.

Picking up along a side edge

With right side facing, and working one whole stitch in from the edge, insert the point of the right needle from front to back between the first and second stitch of the first row. Wind the yarn round the point of the needle and draw the loop through to create a new stitch. Continue along the edge until you have enough stitches.

Picking up along a shaped edge

With right side facing, insert the point of the right needle from front to back into the stitch of the first row below the decreasing stitches. Wind the yarn round the point of the needle and draw the loop through to create a new stitch. Continue along the edge until you have enough stitches.

Binding Off

Binding off is the method of securing the stitches when you have finished
a piece of work. Always bind off in the same stitch as the pattern, unless directed
otherwise. The bound off edge should have the same elasticity as the rest of
the fabric. If you find your edge tends to be too tight, try binding off using a
larger size needle. Ribbing should be bound off quite loosely to keep it elastic.

Bind off in knit stitch

Knit the first two stitches. *Using the point of the left needle, lift the first stitch over the second and drop it off between the two needles. Knit the next stitch, then repeat from * until only one stitch remains on the right needle. Cut the yarn, leaving enough to weave in the end (see page 47, step 2), thread the cut end through the last stitch then drop it off the needle. Pull the yarn firmly to fasten off.

Bind off in purl stitch

Purl the first two stitches. *Using the point of the left needle, lift the first stitch over the second and drop it off between the two needles. Purl the next stitch, then repeat from * until only one stitch remains on the right needle. Cut the yarn, leaving enough to weave in the end (see page 47, step 2), thread the cut end through the last stitch then drop it off the needle. Pull the yarn firmly to fasten off.

Yarn Over Needle

This is a way of making an extra stitch on the needle by making a loop over the needle.
When a yarn over is combined with k2tog on the previous row, the result is an eyelet hole
in the knitted fabric. The abbreviation for "yarn over" needle in a pattern is yo.

Making a yarn over between two knit stitches

Bring the yarn forward as it you were going to purl the next stitch, but then wrap it over the top of the needle in a counterclockwise direction so you can knit the stitch.

Making a yarn over needle between two purl stitches

Wrap the yarn over the top of the needle in a counterclockwise direction, then bring it back under the needle to the front again, so you can purl the next stitch.

Buttonholes

It is useful to be able to work neat buttonholes as badly-made ones can ruin the look of even the most well-made garment. Essentially they are made by binding off a few stitches in one row, then replacing them in the next, leaving a tidy hole.

Making a buttonhole

1 On a right side row, when you get to the start point of the buttonhole bind off the number of stitches specified in the pattern, then continue to the end of the row.

2 On the next row work to the bound off stitches, then turn the work and cast on the same number of stitches you cast off, using the cable method (see page 24).

3 Before placing the last cast on stitch onto the left needle, bring the yarn between the two needles to the front of the work to stop a loop from forming. Turn the work again and finish the row.

Button Up

The technique illustrated here is the two row buttonhole, which is the most versatile, as you can cast off as many or as few stitches as you need to make the relevant size for your button.

The eyelet technique is very quick and neat, but will only work for a limited size of buttonhole. To make an eyelet buttonhole, work to the required position, bring the yarn forward, work the next two stitches together, then work to the end of the row.

Shaping with Decorative Decreasing

Shaping is done either by increasing or decreasing the number of stitches on the needles. Binding off or casting on stitches will produce an abrupt step in the edge, gradual shaping can be produced either by working two or more stitches together (see page 33), making two or more stitches out of one (see page 34–5) or by decorative decreasing. Decorative decreasing is worked in from the edge, so it is designed to show.

Slip one, knit one, pass slipped stitch over—creating a slope to the left

1 Insert the right needle into the first stitch as if to knit it, but slip it onto the right needle without knitting. Knit the next stitch.

2 Using the tip of the left needle, lift the slipped stitch over the stitch you have just knitted, and off the needle. The abbreviation for this in a pattern is sl 1, k1, psso, or sometimes skpo.

Knit two together through the back loop—creating a slope to the left

This is worked in a similar way to k2tog, but knitted through the back of the loops, so twisting the stitches. Insert the tip of the right needle from right to left through the back of the two stitches, then knit them together as one stitch. This is abbreviated in the pattern as k2tog tbl.

Purl two together through back of loops—creating a slope to the left

Again the stitches are knitted through the back of the loops, but this is rather harder to do. Insert the tip of the right needle from left to right through the back of the two stitches, then purl them together as one stitch. This is abbreviated in the pattern as p2tog tbl.

Hitting the Slopes...

When you are working increases and decreases, keep checking your work for mistakes as you go. It is much easier to unravel a few rows and correct any problems as they happen than to go back and do it later.

If required, you can create a more pronounced slope by working three stitches instead of two in each of the techniques above.

Decorative Techniques

Once you have mastered the basic techniques, you can add color and texture to your knitting. Color is added with stripes, or by using intarsia or Fair Isle techniques. Texture is added by working decorative stitches, cables, or knitting with beads. The steps show the basic techniques, but there are further stitch patterns to try in the stitch library on pages 156–157.

Stripes and Blocks

*The easiest way to add more colors to a piece of knitting is by working
stripes in different colors. If the stripes are narrow you can carry the yarn not in
use up the side of the work. If they are quite wide, it is probably better to join the yarn
again further up, as described on page 32. Intarsia introduces colored shapes.*

Carrying the yarn

At the end of the final row in the first color, take the first color yarn over the second color yarn. Continue to work in the second color yarn in the normal way, leaving the first color yarn at the side. Catch the first color as described every two rows, to keep it tight to the edge.

Intarsia

This is a type of color work in which the pattern is made up of large blocks of color. Each block will need its own ball of yarn—a full ball for large blocks, or small amounts wound onto separate bobbins for smaller blocks. As the yarn is not carried across the back all the time, this technique creates a single thickness fabric and is very economical with yarn. Darn in yarn ends at regular intervals, working round blocks of the same color.

Changing Colors

At the first stitch in the new color yarn, insert the tip of the right needle into the stitch, pass the old yarn over the new one, pull the new yarn up and continue knitting. The purl row is worked in exactly the same way. At the end there will be quite a few yarn ends to be tidied away. Weave each end around a block of the same color, working one way first, and then the other way with the next end.

Fair Isle

This type of colorwork is always worked in stockinette stitch, using two or more colors of yarn in each row. The yarn not in use is not cut and rejoined as in intarsia, but carried across the back of the work in a technique known as stranding. If the yarn has to be carried more than three or four stitches, the strand has to be woven in across the back of the fabric as you work. The strands of yarn across the back of the fabric make it double thickness so it is dense and insulating, but the technique does use up a great deal of yarn.

Stranding and Weaving

To weave the strands in, working with the main yarn, insert the tip of the right needle into the stitch. Bring the contrast yarn up from under the one in use, lay it over the right needle, then knit the stitch in the usual way with the main color yarn, dropping the loop of contrast yarn as you work. The contrast yarn will be caught into the back of the fabric. Repeat every three to four stitches, until you need to work with the contrast yarn again. The purl row is worked in the same way.

1 Working with the right side of the work facing, knit the required number of stitches in color one. Drop color one yarn, then insert the tip of the right needle into the next stitch. Pick up color two yarn, taking it over color one yarn, and knit the required number of stitches in color two.

2 Pick up color one yarn from underneath color two yarn and bring it across the back of the stitches you have just made. Keep the strand across the back fairly loose, to keep the elasticity of the fabric. If the stranding is done correctly, the strands will all be neatly horizontal on the back of the work.

Do the Strand

Do not try to carry the yarn over more than three stitches without twisting it with the second color.

Do not pull the yarn too tight when stranding, as this may distort the fabric.

If you have worked this technique correctly, the back of the work will have neat horizontal bars of each yarn being carried.

Ribbing

This stitch combines alternate knit and purl stitches, creating a pattern of vertical bands. It is most often used for borders, particularly at neckband and cuffs, as it creates an elastic edge that will stretch easily. Ribbing can be created by alternating one or more knit and purl stitches each time—the technique is exactly the same. Try to keep the gauge even, as bringing the yarn backwards and forwards as you work can lead to loose knitting.

Single rib

1 With the yarn behind, knit the first stitch then bring the yarn forward between the needles again. Purl the next stitch, then take the yarn back between the needles to repeat.

2 Continue step 1 until all the stitches are knitted. On the next row, the stitches that were knitted are purled and those that were purl stitches are knitted.

Rib Work

Rib does not have to be regular—you could k3 and p1, for instance, in which case the RS and WS will not be identical, as it is in more traditional ribbing.

Ribbing is often knitted on a smaller pair of needles than those used for the main body of a garment, to create a border than fits tighter to the body.

Cables and Bobbles

Cabling and bobble techniques are traditionally associated with Aran knitting, but increasingly are being used as a decorative device in other ways. The cable technique is a method of moving groups of stitches across the material, or crossing one set of stitches over another. The steps here are just for the basic techniques. Bobbles are created by working into the same stitch, turning rows.

Cable 4 Back

1 On a right side row, work to the position of the cable and slip the next two stitches onto a cable needle.

2 With the stitches on the cable needle held at the back of the work, knit the next two stitches from the left needle.

3 Now knit the two stitches from the cable needle to produce the crossover. Leaving the first set of stitches at the back creates a cable that crosses to the right. The abbreviation for this used in a pattern is C4B.

Cable 4 Front

1 On a right side row, work to the position of the cable and slip the next two stitches onto a cable needle.

2 With the stitches on the cable needle held at the front of the work, knit the next two stitches from the left needle.

3 Now knit the two stitches from the cable needle to produce the crossover. Leaving the first set of stitches at the front creates a cable that crosses to the left. The abbreviation for this used in a pattern is C4F.

Twist and Shout

Cable needles with a kink in the middle help to stop the stitches from slipping off.

When working complicated cable patterns, check your work regularly as it is easy to lose track and twist a cable the wrong way.

Cables and twists are traditionally used in Aran knitting, but can also be used in other ways, such as the Cable-Tasseled Scarf by Louise Butt on page 114.

Cables are usually work in stockinette stitch on a reverse stockinette stitch background, so they stand out clearly.

Twist 3 Back

1 On a right side row, work to one stitch before the two knit stitches then slip the next stitch onto a cable needle.

2 With the stitch on the cable needle held at the back of the work, knit the next two stitches from the left needle.

3 Now purl the stitch from the cable needle to produce a twist to the right. The abbreviation for this used in a pattern is T3B.

Pattern Play

Twist stitches are usually worked with fewer stitches than cables, so often a cable needle is not required.

With this techniques the stitches can move across the background to create zigzags and diagonals, rather than just crossing backwards and forwards on themselves as cables do.

Twists and cables are often combined with bobbles in traditional Aran knitting. The techniques for making a bobble are shown on page 53.

Twist 3 Front

1 On a right side row, work to one stitch before the two knit stitches, then slip the next two stitches onto a cable needle.

2 With the stitches on the cable needle held at the front of the work, purl the next stitch from the left needle.

3 Now knit the two stitches from the cable needle to produce a twist to the left. The abbreviation for this used in a pattern is T3F.

Beyond the Basics

Aran knitting may look complicated, but once you have mastered cables, twists, and bobbles—which are all quite simple in themselves—you will have all the basic techniques you need to tackle even the most complicated Aran pattern.

Just varying the number of stitches and the position and direction of the cable or twist gives a wide variety of different effects.

Twisting 1, 2 or 4 stitches is carried out in exactly the same way as described here for 3 stitches. The twisting technique is used in Kate Buchanan's Mable Cable Hat on page 144.

Bobbles

1 On a right side row, knit to the position of the bobble. Knit into the front, back, front, back and front again of the next stitch, and slip the stitch off the left needle so the five new stitches are on the right needle.

2 Turn the work so that the wrong side is facing and purl the five bobble stitches, then turn again and knit them. Repeat the last two rows once more, thus making four rows in stockinette stitch over the bobble stitches.

3 With the right side facing, use the tip of the left needle to lift the second, third, fourth and fifth bobble stitches, in order, over the first one on the needle so one stitch remains. Continue knitting the row.

On the Ball

It can be hard to get a row of bobbles even at first, but keep practicing and try to work them fairly loosely, which may help.

There are many ways to create a bobble, all of them quite similar—these steps show the basic technique. The exact method needed to create a particular bobble is usually detailed in the pattern.

The more stitches and rows you work, the bigger the final bobble.

Knitting with Beads

Adding beads is a great way to incorporate color and texture into a knitted garment. Usually the beads are spaced out over the fabric, either in a random way or to create a pattern on the surface. The beads should be added to the ball of yarn before you begin, as after you start knitting you can only add more beads by unraveling the whole ball and adding from the other end, or cutting the yarn. For this reason, it is a good idea to add more beads that you think you will need.

On a right side row, knit to where the bead is to be placed. Bring the yarn to the front between the needles and push a bead down close to the work, in front of the next stitch to be worked. Place the tip of the right needle into the next stitch as if to purl, but slip it onto the right needle without working. Take the yarn back through the needles and continue knitting the row.

Working with beaded yarn

The quickest way to thread beads onto the yarn is to use a needle and sewing cotton. Thread the needle with a loop of sewing cotton, then thread the end of the yarn through the loop. Thread the beads onto the needle and down onto the yarn.

Bead the Way

When choosing your beads, make sure they have a large enough central hole to take the yarn you are using, but not so large that they will slide around too much as you work.

Match the size of the beads to the thickness of the yarn for a more subtle effect.

Beads that tone with the yarn add sparkle and texture. Contrasting beads give a more dramatic effect as they will stand out against the fabric, adding texture, sparkle and color.

Avoid beads that are too heavy as they will cause the yarn to sag, so the bead will not sit tight to the knitted fabric.

Traditional beading covered the fabric with beads, closely clustered together so little of the underlying yarn showed. Modern designs more often create a pattern with the beads on the surface of the knitting. This uses less beads and means the final item is lighter in weight.

Finishing

A proper finish will give your design a clean,
polished, and professional appearance. From blocking
and ironing to attaching seams, these final steps
to knitting can make a lasting impression.

Blocking

This is the careful pinning out of separate pieces of knitting before ironing to ensure they are the correct shape and measurements. This should always be done before joining seams. Blocking is very useful for smoothing out multicolor knitting, which often looks uneven, and for adjusting slightly the size or shape of a garment without re-knitting it.

For blocking and ironing you will need a flat, padded surface covered with a clean cloth—an ironing board with a thick towel fastened over it will do. A more professional blocking board is easy to make—just cover a large piece of wood with a layer of old towels or quilt batting, then cover in cotton gingham fabric, taking it round to the back and stapling into place. The geometric lines of the gingham will help you get edges straight. You will also need long dressmaker's pins with large colored heads, an iron and a pressing cloth.

To block, arrange the pieces of knitting wrong-side up on the padded surface. Place pins at intervals of around 1 in. (2.5 cm), angling them through the edge of the knitting into the padding, avoiding ribbed sections. Check that the measurements are correct and that the lines of stitches are straight in both horizontal and vertical directions. Re-pin if necessary to achieve the correct size and shape, stretching or easing slightly if required so that the outline forms a smooth edge between the pins.

Ironing and Damp Finishing

Each pinned-out section of knitting is ironed or damp-finished to give a smooth finish and help it to hold its shape. The characteristics of yarns vary greatly, and information on individual yarns is usually given on the ball band. If in doubt about ironing, always try ironing the gauge swatch first to avoid spoiling the actual garment. For wool, cotton, linen, and other natural yarns use a damp cloth, steam thoroughly, but avoid letting the iron rest on the work.

Some types of knitting or parts of a garment are best left unironed, even if the yarn is suitable for ironing. These include ribbing and cable and texture patterns as ironing may flatten the texture and blur the details, and can make the ribbing lose its elasticity. Damp finishing is more suitable in these cases. It is also suitable for fluffy and synthetic yarns—do not iron yarns that are 100% synthetic. For yarns that are a mixture (containing some natural fibers), use a cool iron over a dry cloth.

To iron, cover the pinned-out pieces with a damp or dry cloth, depending on the yarn. Check that the iron is the correct heat, then iron evenly and lightly, lifting the iron up and down to avoid dragging the knitted material underneath. Do not iron the ribbed edges. After ironing, remove a few pins. If the edge stays flat, take out all the pins and leave the knitting to dry before removing it from the flat surface. If the edge curls when a few pins are removed, re-pin it and leave to dry with the pins in position. After joining the completed pieces of knitting, iron the seams lightly on the wrong side, using the same method as before but without pinning.

To damp finish, lay pieces on a damp (colorfast) towel, then roll them up together and leave for about an hour to allow the knitting to absorb the moisture from the towel. Unwrap, lay the damp towel on a flat surface and place the pieces on top of it. Ease the pieces into shape and pin as explained in Blocking, on page 58, but do not iron. Lay another damp towel over the top, pat all over firmly to establish contact, then leave to dry.

Pressing Matters

Always check the information on the ball band before ironing—some yarns may not be able to withstand the heat.

Never try to iron heavily textured patterns or bobbles as this will blur the details—you may be able to damp finish them instead, but if in any doubt leave well enough alone.

Fluffy yarns, such as mohair, can be brushed with a fine brush to finish them—particularly after the item has been washed.

Finishing

*This is the final stage in creating your garment. Badly stitched seams
can ruin a lovely piece of knitting, so it is worth spending a bit of time to get it right.
Make sure everything is blocked before you begin to sew.*

Mattress stitch

This stitch makes an invisible seam and is especially good for matching stripes, as it is worked from the right side.

Joining a side seam

With the right side facing, lay the two pieces to be joined flat on a surface edge to edge. Thread a yarn needle and attach the end of the yarn on the back of one side, then bring the needle to the front between the first and second stitch in from the edge. Pass the needle through the loops of the first two rows on that side, then across and through two loops of the directly opposite two rows on the other piece. Bring the needle back to the first piece, inserting it in the same hole it came out of and then under the two loops of the next two rows. Work several stitches in this zig zag manner before pulling the yarn tight to check the seam. Do not pull the yarn too tight—make sure the elasticity of the seam is the same as on the rest of the knitted fabric.

Joining a side to a top or bottom edge

Start as for the side seam. Bring the needle through to the front between the first and second stitch in from the side edge and pick up one loop of the first row on that side, then across and through the middle of the first stitch directly opposite on the other piece, coming up through the middle of the next stitch. Since a stitch is wider than it is long you will have to work three rows to two stitches. Work several stitches in this zigzag manner before pulling the yarn tight to check the seam. Do not pull the yarn too tight—make sure the elasticity of the seam is the same as on the rest of the knitted fabric.

Joining bound off or cast on edges

In this method, the yarn will show on the front of the fabric, so use a yarn matching the work. Secure the end of the yarn as for the side seam. Bring the needle out in the center of the first stitch in the row below the edge and then across and through the middle of the first stitch directly opposite on the other piece, coming up through the middle of the next stitch. Make sure the elasticity of the seam is the same as on the rest of the knitted fabric.

Backstitch seam

This seam is very strong, but also quite bulky. You work on the wrong side of the fabric, so it is also quite difficult to match patterns.

Working a backstitch seam

Pin the pieces to be joined, right sides together and matching rows. Thread a yarn needle and secure the yarn end by taking it through the first pair of stitches a couple of times. Make a double-length stitch on the reverse then bring the needle through to the front. Insert the needle into the work just behind where it came out and make another double-length stitch on the back. Insert the needle at the end of the short stitch showing on the front and make another double-length stitch on the back. Continue in this way to create an even row of small stitches right next to each other on the front, with double-length stitches overlapping on the reverse.

Flat seam

A flat seam is created by overcasting the two edges, working on the two edge stitches. When it is opened out the seam will be flat, which makes it ideal for sewing on collars or button bands.

Working a Flat Seam

Place the pieces to be joined, right sides together—they can be pinned in place, or just held together between fingers and thumb. Thread a yarn needle and secure the yarn end by taking it through the first pair of stitches a couple of times. Insert the needle from the back through the edge stitches of both pieces. Pull the yarn through, then take the next stitch. Continue in this way to the end of the seam.

Correcting Mistakes

Even the most experienced knitter makes the
odd mistake, but there are a few things you can do to
try to avoid them, or to make sure you see the error
before you have worked too many more rows. First, try out
the stitch pattern in some spare yarn beforehand, so you
become familiar with the feel of the pattern before you get
going. While working the garment, check back frequently
to make sure the pattern has been worked correctly. It is
far easier and less frustrating to unravel just one or two
rows than to have to repeat half a dozen!

Dropped Stitch

Fear not! Dropping a stitch is perhaps the most common mistake made in knitting. If you have only worked a row above the lost stitch, it can easily be picked up.

Picking up stitch on a knit row

1 Knit along the row until you reach the dropped stitch. Pick up the stitch from front to back with the point of the right hand needle then pick up the horizontal strand above it.

Drop the Issue

If dropped stitches have been allowed to run down several rows they will create a "ladder" in the knitted fabric. See Louise Butt's creative use of this effect in the Drop-Stitch Cardigan on page 75 and the Cable Shrug on page 78!

Avoid leaving your work in the middle of a row, as this is often when a dropped stitch occurs.

2 Insert the tip of the left hand needle into the dropped stitch from back to front and lift it over the strand and off the needle.

3 The stitch has now been recreated, but it is the wrong way round on the right hand needle. To turn it the correct way, insert the tip of the left hand needle into it from front to back and slip it over to the left needle. You can then continue to knit the row as normal.

Picking up stitch on a purl row

1 Purl along the row until you reach the dropped stitch. Pick up the stitch from back to front with the point of the right hand needle, then pick up the horizontal strand above the lost stitch.

2 Insert the tip of the left hand needle into the dropped stitch from front to back and lift it over the strand and off the needle. The stitch has now been recreated on the right hand needle so just slip it over to the left needle. You can then continue to purl the row as normal.

Picking up a stitch over several rows

If you don't notice the dropped stitch immediately, it may have run further, forming a ladder. Working with the knit side facing you, insert a crochet hook into the front of the stitch, then catch the horizontal bar above with the hook and pull it through the stitch. Continue in this way until you reach the needle, then put the stitch on the left hand needle and continue as before.

Unraveling

If you have worked several rows above the lost stitch, the yarn will be pulled tight across the gap further up, so there will be no spare yarn to recreate the stitch. The only thing to do here is to unravel your work to the point at which you dropped the stitch.

Unraveling a single row

1 The best way to unravel a single row is stitch by stitch. Insert the tip of the left hand needle from front to back into the center of the stitch below the one on the right hand needle.

2 Pull the right hand needle back a little to drop the higher stitch off, then pull the yarn free. Continue in this way until you reach the end of the row.

Come Undone

Unraveling is also the best answer if you have made a major mistake in the pattern, rather than trying to change things in small sections and possibly damaging the yarn. It may seem like a lot of work, but better to correct a problem now than to be looking at a mistake in an otherwise beautifully-knitted garment for years to come!

Unraveling several rows

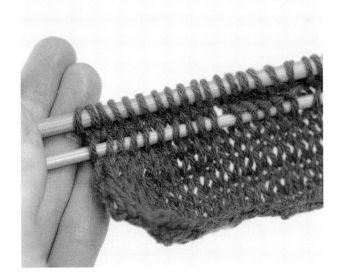

First use a spare smaller gauge needle and slide it into the knitting to pick up the row of stitches just below the error. Remove the needle from the top of the work and gently pull to unravel back to the stitches on the lower needle.

Fashion

These garments are as much fun to knit as they
are to wear. From a demure Cap-Sleeve Tunic to
a pretty Cable Shrug, an exquisite Drop-stitch Cardigan
to a Stripy Joe sweater, the easy-going designs in this
chapter are both classic and contemporary.

Cap-Sleeve Tunic

Designed by Sîan Luyken, this flattering and elegant tunic makes a versatile summer knit, which can be worn with the lace panel at the back or the front. The yarn contains enough elastic to make it easy to knit and comfortable to wear.

Materials

Yarn

Calmer by Rowan, 1¾oz/50g ball, each approx 175 yd/160 m (75% cotton, 25% acrylic/ microfiber)

4 (4, 5, 5, 5) balls in Powder Puff 482

Needles and extras

2 pairs US 9 (5.5 mm) needles

2 stitch markers

2 stitch holders

Gauge

24 sts and 32 rows to 4 in. (10 cm) over stockinette stitch, on US 9 (5.5 mm) needles. If necessary change needle size to obtain this gauge.

Sizes and Measurements

To fit: bust 32 (34, 36, 38, 40) in. [81 (86, 91, 97, 102) cm]

Actual measurements: bust 30½ (33½, 35½, 37½, 39½) in. [76.5 (83, 88, 93, 98) cm]; length 24 (25½, 27¼, 28 3/4, 30¼) in. [60 (63, 68, 72, 75) cm]

Front

Using thumb cast on, cast on 96 (104, 110, 116, 122) sts.

Row 1 (WS): Purl.

Row 2: K47 (51, 54, 57, 60), yf, k1, yf, k1, yf, k to end.

Row 3: P47 (51, 54, 57, 60), p2tog three times, p to end.

These two rows form the lace pattern. Continue this pattern throughout the garment.

Work 7 (13, 13, 15, 15) rows.

Dec one st at each end of next row and every following 10th (8th, 8th, 8th, 8th) row until 82 (86, 92, 98, 102) sts remain.

Work 9 (7, 9, 15, 7) rows.

Then inc 1 st at each end of next and every following 10th (6th, 8th, 8th, 8th) row until 92 (100, 106, 112, 118) sts.

Work 8 (14, 8, 8, 6) rows, ending on a WS row.

Shape armhole:

Bind off 10 (10, 11, 12, 11) at beginning of next two rows.

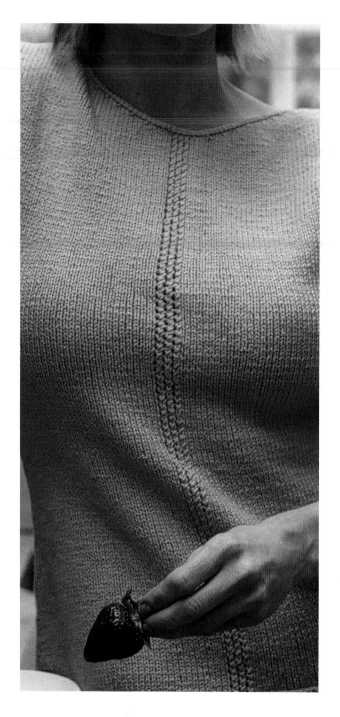

Work 0 (2, 0, 0, 0) rows, placing stitch markers 3 sts in from either end on last row.

At stitch markers, M1 on next and every alt row until 118 (124, 134, 144, 156) sts, ending on a WS row.

Shape shoulder:

Work each side separately.

Next row: K56 (57, 68, 63, 67), yf, sl 1, turn, yf, sl 1. You have formed a wrap around the last unworked st of the row. Repeat this wrap at the end of each short row.

Next row: P52 (53, 59, 62, 69), turn, wrapping last unworked st.

Continue working back and forth, working 4 (4, 4, 5, 5) fewer sts at sleeve end and 3 sts fewer on neck end until 3 (4, 3, 6, 5) sts remain, ending on WS. Break yarn and rejoin to work other shoulder, mirroring the shaping.

Break yarn again, and rejoin at end with RS facing. Knit along whole row, picking up and knitting the wraps together with their stitches.

Next row: P32 (32, 36, 40, 45) sts, bind off 54 (60, 62, 64, 66) sts, purl to end of row. Place remaining sts on stitch holders or loop of waste yarn.

Back

Work as for front, but omitting lace panel.

Finishing

Weave in ends and block and press as described on pages 58–9 to stop the stockinette stitch curling. If the edges still curl, steam block again once you've made up the tunic. Place the right-hand shoulders of both sides back onto US 9 (5.5 mm) needles. Hold together with WS facing out. Using a third needle, knit the first stitch of each needle together. Repeat, and pass the first stitch over. Continue until one stitch remains, break yarn and pull through. This is called a three-needle bind off.

Join the left-hand shoulder seam the same way, making sure that RS are facing inwards. Turn knitting the right way around, and join side seams using mattress stitch. Weave in the ends and steam seams. If necessary, pin the edges and do a second block.

Drop-Stitch Cardigan

This really pretty cardigan designed by Louise Butt boasts an unusual drop-stitch pattern that is so simple even a beginner can make it. It would look great over a plain t-shirt during the daytime, or over an attractive sleeveless tank for an evening occasion.

Materials

Yarn
Luxury Soft Cotton by Sirdar, 1¾oz/50g ball, each approx 103 yd/95 m (100% cotton)
6 (7, 8, 9, 10) balls in Raspberry 663

Needles and extras
1 pair of US 6 (4 mm) needles
1 pair of US 8 (5 mm) needles
Yarn needle

Gauge
22 sts and 28 rows to 4 in. (10 cm) over stockinette stitch, on US 6 (4 mm) needles. If necessary change needle size to obtain this gauge.

Special Abbreviations
dr1st = Drop 1 st off needle without knitting, so that it will unravel to the cast on edge.
kfb = knit into front and back of st.

Sizes and Measurements

To fit: bust 32–34 (36–38, 40–42, 44–46, 48–50) in. [82–86.5 (91.5–97, 101.5–107, 112–117, 122–127) cm]

Actual measurements: bust 37½ (41, 44½, 47½, 51) in. [94 (102, 110.5, 119, 127.5) cm]; length 22 (22½, 23½, 24, 24½) in. [56 (57, 60, 61, 62.5) cm]

Back

Cast on 89 (97, 105, 113, 121) sts using US 6 (4 mm) needles.
Starting with a knit row, St st for 15 (15, 15.5, 15.5, 16) in. [38 (38, 39.5, 39.5, 40.5) cm] ending on a WS row.

Shape armhole:
Next row (RS): Bind off 5 sts at beg of row, k to end.
Next row (WS): Bind off 5 sts purlwise at beg of row, p to end.
Continue in St st until knitting measures 22 (22½, 23½, 24, 24½) in. [56 (57, 60, 61, 62.5) cm] ending on a RS row.
Next row (WS): P3, dr1st, *p7, dr1st; rep from * to last 3 sts, p3.
Bind off loosely.
Tease the dropped stitches so that they unravel to the cast-on row.

Right front

Cast on 43 (47, 52, 55, 60) sts, using US 6 (4 mm) needles.
Work in St st for 13 (13, 13½, 13½, 14) in. [33 (33, 34.5, 34.5, 35.5) cm] ending on a WS row**.

Shape neck:

Next row (RS): K2tog, k to end.
Work the next 3 rows in St st.
Rep last 4 rows, incorporating dropped sts as follows: On the 9th (5th, 2nd, 5th, 2nd) decrease row, k2tog, dr1st, k to end of row. AT THE SAME TIME when knitting measures 15 (15, 15½, 15½, 16) in. [38 (38, 39.5, 39.5, 40.5) cm, on a WS row, bind off 5 sts purlwise, p to end of row.
Cont with 4-row neck decreases and on every foll eighth dec row, k2tog, dr1st, k to end of row.
Cont with 4-row neck decreases until right front measures 22 (22½, 23½, 24, 24½) in. [56 (57, 60, 61, 62.5) cm], ending on a RS row.
Next row (WS): P3, *dr1st, p7; rep from * to end of row. (If 7 sts don't remain after last dropped st, just p to end.)
Bind off loosely.
Tease the dropped stitches so that they unravel to the cast-on row.

Left front

Rep as for right front to **.

Shape neck:

Next row (RS): K to last 2 sts, k2tog.
Work the next 3 rows in St st.
Rep last 4 rows, incorporating dropped sts as follows: On the 9th (5th, 2nd, 5th, 2nd) decrease row, k to last 3 sts, dr1st, k2tog. AT THE SAME TIME when knitting measures 15 (15, 15½, 15½, 16) in. [38 (38, 39.5, 39.5, 40.5) cm on a RS row, cast off 5 sts, k to end of row.
Cont with 4-row neck decreases and on every foll

eighth dec row, k to last 3 sts, dr1st, k2tog to end of row.
Cont with 4-row neck decreases until left front measures 22 (22½, 23½, 24, 24½) in. [56 (57, 60, 61, 62.5) cm], ending on a RS row.
Next row (WS): P until 7 sts have been worked since last dropped st, dr1st, *p7, dr1st; rep from * to last 3 sts, p3.
Bind off loosely.
Tease the dropped stitches so that they unravel to the cast-on row.

Sleeves (Make both the same)

Cast on 65 (81, 83, 89, 95) sts, using US 6 (4 mm) needles.
Work in St st for 2 rows.
Next row: Kfb, k to last st, kfb.
Next row: Purl.
Rep last 2 rows 5 times more: 77 (93, 95, 101, 107) sts.
Cont in St st until sleeve measures 4 (4, 5, 5, 6) in. [10 (10, 12.5, 12.5, 15) cm] ending on a RS row.
Next row (WS): P10 (14, 15, 14, 13) sts, dr1st, *p7, dr1st; rep from * to last 10 (14, 15, 14, 13) sts, p to end of row.
Bind off loosely.
Tease the dropped stitches so that they unravel to the cast-on row.

Finishing

Darn in all ends. Join shoulder seams.

Make front border:

Starting at base of right front and with right side facing, with US 8 (5 mm) needles pick up and k one st for every two rows of knitting, then pick up and k1 st for every bound-off st along back, then pick up and k1 st for every two rows down left front.
Starting with a p row, work 6 rows in St st.
Bind off.

These 6 rows of reverse St st will curl on themselves. Join side seams, then join sleeve seams and attach to armhole edges.

Details, details, details...

It may seem a bit scary to drop stitches, but don't worry—this will not cause the garment to fall apart! The "ladder" effect is a great way to create a really simple but effective openwork design.

The sleeve edges and base of the cardigan will curl naturally to match the reverse stockinette stitch edging along the front border.

This is a great project for knitting-on-the-go, as it is small and easy to carry around, plus you don't have to worry too much about dropped stitches!

If you use the yarn end from the center of the ball, rather than the outer end, the ball does not roll around as much as you work—so it will not pick up any bits of dirt or fluff that may be lying around.

Cable Shrug

Update the traditional cable stitch pattern on this flare-sleeved shrug, by dropping a line of stitches on either side of the cable. Louise Butt's simple cable pattern offers a snazzy and fashionable garment, but the ladders created by the dropped stitch create a light autumn cover-up.

Materials

Yarn

Cashmerino Aran by Debbie Bliss, 1¾oz/50g ball, each 98 yd/90 m (55% merino wool, 33% microfiber, 12% cashmere) 5 (6, 7) balls in 300602

Needles and extras

1 pair of US 8 (5 mm) needles
1 cable needle

Gauge

18 sts and 24 rows to 4 in. (10 cm) over stockinette stitch on US 8 (5 mm) needles. If necessary change needles to obtain this gauge.

Special Abbreviations

C6F = Slip 3 sts onto cable needle, hold at front of work, k3 sts from left needle, then k sts off cable needle.

dr1st = Drop 1 st off needle without knitting it so that it will unravel to the cast on edge.

m1 = make 1 st, pick up loop before the next stitch and knit into the back of it.

Sizes and Measurements

To fit: bust 32-36 (36-40, 40-44) in. [81-91.5 (91.5-101.5, 101.5-111.5) cm]

First cuff

Cast on 78 (94, 110) sts.

Row 1: K2, p10, *k6, p10; rep from * to last 2 sts, k2.

Row 2: P2, k10, *p6, k10; rep from * to last 2 sts, p2.

Row 3: K2, p10, *C6F, p10, rep from * to last 2 sts, k2.

Row 4: As row 2.

Row 5: As row 1.

Row 6: P2, k4, k2tog, k4, *p6, k4, k2tog, k4; rep from * to last 2 sts, p2.

Row 7: K2, p9, *k6, p9; rep from * to last 2 sts, k2.

Row 8: P2, k9, *p6, k9; rep from * to last 2 sts, p2.

Row 9: K2, p9, *C6F, p9, rep from * to last 2 sts, k2.

Row 10: As row 8.

Row 11: As row 7.

Row 12: P2, k4, k2tog, k3, *p6, k4, k2tog, k3; rep from * to last 2 sts, p2.

Row 13: K2, p8, *k6, p8; rep from * to last 2 sts, k2.

Row 14: P2, k8, * p6, k8; rep from * to last 2 sts, p2.

Row 15: K2, p8, *C6F, p8; rep from * to last 2 sts, k2.

Row 16: As row 14.

Row 17: As row 13.

Row 18: P2, k3, k2tog, k3, *p6, k3, k2tog, k3; rep from * to last 2 sts, p2.

Row 19: K2, p7, *k6, p7; rep from * to last 2 sts, k2.

Row 20: P2, k7, *p6, k7; rep from * to last 2 sts, p2.

Row 21: K2, p7, *C6F, p7; rep from * to last 2 sts, k2.

Row 22: As row 20.

Row 23: As row 19.

Row 24: P2, k3, k2tog, k2, *p6, k3, k2tog, k2; rep from * to last 2 sts, p2.

Row 25: K2, p6, *k6, p6; rep from * to last 2 sts, k2.

Row 26: P2, k6, *p6, k6; rep from * to last 2 sts, p2.

Row 27: K2, p6, *C6F, p6; rep from * to last 2 sts, k2.

Row 28: As row 26.

Row 29: As row 25.

Row 30: P2, k2, k2tog, k2, *p6, k2, k2tog, k2; rep from * to last 2 sts, p2.

Start straight shrug:

Row 31: **K2, p5, *k6, p5; rep from * to last 2 sts, k2.

Row 32: P2, k5, *p6, k5; rep from * to last 2 sts, p2.

Row 33: K2, p5, *C6F, p5; rep from * to last 2 sts, k2.

Row 34: P2, k5, *p6, k5; rep from * to last 2 sts, p2.

Row 35: K2, p5, *k6, p5; rep from * to last 2 sts, k2.

Row 36: P2, k5, *p6, k5; rep from * to last 2 sts, p2***.

Rep from ** to *** until work measures 50 (54, 58) in. [127 (137, 147) cm]
Next row: As row 31.

Work second cuff.
Row 1: P2, k2, m1, k3, *p6, k2, m1, k3; rep from * to last 2 sts, p2.
Row 2: K2, p6, *C6F, p6; rep from * to last 2 sts, k2.
Row 3: P2, k6, *p6, k6; rep from * to last 2 sts, p2.
Row 4: K2, p6, * k6, p6; rep from * to last 2 sts, k2.
Row 5: As row 3.
Row 6: As row 4.
Row 7: P2, k3, m1, k3, *p6, k3, m1, k3; rep from * to last 2 sts, p2.
Row 8: K2, p7, *C6F, p7; rep from * to last 2 sts, k2.
Row 9: P2, k7, * p6, k7; rep from * to last 2 sts, p2.
Row 10: K2, p7, *k6, p7; rep from * to last 2 sts, k2.
Row 11: As row 9.
Row 12: As row 10.
Row 13: P2, k3, m1, k4, *p6, k3, m1, k4; rep from * to last 2 sts, p2.
Row 14: K2, p8, *C6F, p8; rep from * to last 2 sts, k2.
Row 15: P2, k8, *p6, k8; rep from * to last 2 sts, p2.
Row 16: K2, p8, *k6, p8; rep from * to last 2 sts, k2.
Row 17: As row 15.
Row 18: As row 16.
Row 19: P2, k4, m1, k4, *p6, k4, m1, k4; rep from * to last 2 sts, p2.
Row 20: K2, p9, *C6F, p9; rep from * to last 2 sts, k2.
Row 21: P2, k9, *p6, k9; rep from * to last 2 sts, p2.
Row 22: K2, p9, *k6, p9; rep from * to last 2 sts, k2.
Row 23: As row 21.
Row 24: As row 22.
Row 25: P2, k4, m1, k5, *p6, k4, m1, k5; rep from * to last 2 sts, p2.
Row 26: K2, p10, * C6F, p10; rep from * to last 2 sts, k2.
Row 27: P2, k10, *p6, k10; rep from * to last 2 sts, p2.
Row 28: K2, p10, *k6, p10; rep from * to last 2 sts, k2.
Row 29: As row 27.
Row 30: As row 28.
Bind off all sts loosely WHILE following this drop st patt: p2, k1, dr1st, k6, dr1st, k1, *p6, k1, dr1st, k6, dr1st, k1; rep from * to last 2 sts, p2.
Tease the dropped stitches so that they unravel to the cast-on row.

Finishing
From each cuff measure 18 (19, 20) in. [45 (48.5, 50.5) cm] and sew up seams from cuff to this point.

Style Guide
Try on one sleeve after you have sewn the seam to check that the stitched part is a comfortable length before sewing the other side.

The ends of the sleeves are gently flared, but you could gather them with shirring elastic or even a knitted cord if you prefer a tighter cuff at the wrist.

When unraveling the dropped stitches, tease them gently down to the cast-on row. They will stop naturally there so you don't need to worry about the whole garment falling apart.

Like many of the garments in this book, this one has alternative instructions for different sizes. When you have decided which size you are going to make, it is a good idea to go through the pattern before you start and highlight all the instructions that refer to that size, so you don't get confused as you work.

Seaweed Wrap

Designed by Sîan Luyken, this versatile wrap can be worn with your arms through the holes and the long side either wrapped around your neck, or folded and pinned with a pretty brooch. Alternatively, you could wear it as a scarf with the long end passed through a hole.

Materials

Yarn

Mohair by Colinette, 3½oz/100g skein, each approx 190 yd/175 m (78% mohair, 13% wool, 9% nylon)

2 skeins in Monet

Needles and extras

1 pair US 15 (10 mm) needles

1 15/M (10mm) crochet hook

Gauge

13 sts and 12 rows to 4 in. (10 cm) in pattern, on US 15 (10 mm) needles. If necessary change needle size to obtain this gauge.

Sizes and Measurements

To fit: bust 32–34 (36–38, 40–42) in. [81–86 (91–97, 102–107) cm]

Actual measurements: width 20 (25, 28½) in. [50 (63, 71.5) cm]; **length** 42 (48½, 56) in. [105 (121.5, 140) cm]

Wrap

Cast on 65 (81, 93) stitches.

Row 1 (RS): K2tog, *(k1, yf, k1) all into one stitch, sl 1, k2tog, psso; repeat from * until 3 sts from end, (k1, yf, k1) all into one stitch, sl 1, k1, psso.

Row 2: Purl.

These two rows form pattern. Continue working straight in pattern for 50 (60, 70) rows.

Shape armhole:

Work in pattern for 38 (41, 49) stitches, bind off 12 (15, 16) sts, continue in pattern to end of row.

Work both sides of armhole separately, using second ball of yarn to work rows on alternate sides.

Next row: Purl.

Dec 1 st at armhole end of next 2 (2, 3) alt rows.

Work straight for 2 (2, 2) rows.

Inc 1 st at armhole end for next 2 (2, 3) rows.

Work 1 (1, 0) row.

Close armhole:

Next row (WS): P to armhole edge, cast on 12 (15, 16) sts, p to end.

Continue in pattern for 36 (44, 50) rows, then make second armhole. After closing second armhole, work 14 (16, 20) rows. Bind off loosely.

Finishing

With 15/M (10mm) hook, crochet a chain around armhole.

Stripy Joe

Kate Buchanan's quick-to-knit sweater in funky stripes can be completed over a long weekend! The yarn is used double which, on big needles, produces a garment with a lovely drape. The bell-shaped sleeves can be gathered at the wrist or left flared.

Materials

Yarn
Country Style DK by Sirdar, 3½oz/100g ball, each approx 346 yd/318 m (15% wool, 40% nylon, 45% acrylic)

4 (6, 6, 6, 6, 6) balls in Raspberry 539 (A)

2 (3, 3, 3, 3, 3) balls in Rosehip 527 (B)

2 (3, 3, 3, 3, 3) balls in Bilberry 501 (C)

Needles and extras
1 × US 11 (8 mm) circular needle

Darning needle

Gauge
14 sts and 17 rows to 4 in. (10 cm) over stockinette stitch, on US 11 (8 mm) needles using DK yarn double.

Stripe Out!
The stripes are created by alternating between two colorways of yarn: A and B are used together to make AB, and A and C make AC. To make this easier, wind up a grapefruit sized ball of each color combination before you start. You'll need six to eight of these sized balls to complete the garment.

Sizes and Measurements

To fit: bust 32 (34, 36, 38, 40, 42) in. [81 (86, 91, 97, 102, 107) cm]

Actual measurements: bust 33½ (36, 38, 40½, 43, 45½) in. [84 (90, 95, 101, 107, 113) cm]; **length** 19½ (21, 22, 23½, 25, 26) in. [49 (52, 55, 58.5, 62, 65) cm]; **incorporated sleeve** 18½in (46 cm).

Sweater
Using AC and US 11 (8 mm) needles, cast on 56 (58, 60, 62, 64, 66) sts.

Work from sleeve cuff: K into the back loop of every st.

Next row: Purl.

Join AB onto AC. With AB, k2, *yo, k2tog; rep from * to last 2 sts, yo 0 (1, 0, 1, 0, 1) time, k2.

Next row: Purl.

From now on, work St st. Starting with AC, work 2 rows then change to AB for 2 rows. Alternate colors every 2 rows throughout pattern.

Dec 1 at each end of every 10th (10th, 10th, 13th, 20th, 14th) row for 40 rows: 48 (50, 52, 56, 60, 64) sts.

Continue to work straight for a further 30 rows. Reduce or increase number of rows here to change length of sleeve if desired. Sleeve measures 17¼ in. (43 cm) in length from cast on edge.

Shape underarm:

Cast on 4 (4, 6, 6, 7, 7) sts at beg of next 4 rows, making sure that you carry the yarn not being used at back of work: 64 (66, 76, 80, 88, 92) sts.

Work body:

Cast on 30 (34, 33, 35, 35, 38) sts at beg of next 2 rows: 124 (134, 142, 150, 158, 168) sts.

Next row: Knit.

Next row: K5, p to last 5 sts, k5. This will create a garter st edge along bottom of front and back. Continue garter st edge throughout pattern for front and back of body.

Repeat last 2 rows until 16 (16, 16, 18, 18, 20) rows have been worked from beg of body section.

Work back neckline:

K60 (65, 69, 73, 77, 82), k2tog, turn. Leave rem sts on needle.

Dec 1 st at this edge for next 3 (3, 5, 5, 7, 7) rows.

Work 30 (32, 34, 36, 38, 40) rows of St st, maintaining 5 sts garter edge on one side (hem edge).

Inc 1 st at neckline edge for next 4 (4, 6, 6, 8, 8) rows.

Work 1 row then cut yarn, leaving sts on needle.

Work front neckline:

Join yarns at beg of neckline. Maintaining stripe pattern, cast off 6 (6, 6, 8, 8, 8) sts.

Dec 1 st at neckline edge for next 5 (5, 5, 5, 7, 7) rows.

Work 26 (28, 34, 36, 38, 40) rows St st, maintaining 5 sts garter edge on one side (hem edge).

Inc 1 st at neckline edge for next 5 (5, 5, 5, 7, 7) rows.

Next row: K5, purl to end of row.

Cast on 6 (6, 6, 8, 8, 8) sts, k to end of row.

Next row: k5, purl across front then purl sts from back to last 5 sts, k5.

Join other yarn color.

Work 14 (14, 14, 16, 16, 18) rows, maintaining 5 sts garter edge on each side.

Bind off 30 (34, 33, 35, 35, 38) sts at beg of next 2 rows.

Bind off 4 (4, 6, 6, 7, 7) sts at beg of next 4 rows.

Work St st for 30 rows.

Inc 1 st at each end of next and every foll 10th (10th, 10th, 15th, 20th, 0) row for 31 rows.

Work 9 rows.

Next row: Knit.

Next row: P2, *yo, p2tog; rep from * to last 2st, yo 0 (1, 0, 1, 0, 1) times, p2.

Next row: K into back loop of every st.

Bind off purlwise.

Collar

With AC and starting at top of shoulder, pick up 74 (74, 80, 86, 92, 96) sts around neckline edge.

Work 4 rows garter st, alternating yarn colors every 2 rows.

Bind off loosely.

Finishing

Join side and sleeve seams. Join collar seam. Measure 2 × 40 in. (100 cm) lengths of yarn in each color. With one strand of each color together, hold one end firmly and twist the other tightly. Fold in half, pinch in the middle and let go of the ends so strands twist together to form a cord. Tie a knot in each end and repeat with other 3 strands. Weave cord in and out of eyelets by cuff. Gather and tie with a bow.

Make the Best of your Knitting

When there are several stitches cast on or bound off in the pattern, carry the yarn color not being used along the back of the work by twisting it with the yarn in use every 3 sts as you would when using the Fair Isle stranding technique (see page 46–7).

This pullover is knitted all in one piece, beginning at one sleeve cuff and working across the entire garment to the other cuff, with the collar knitted on at the end by picking up stitches around the neckline. There are no sleeves to set in—all you have to do is join the side, sleeve and collar seams.

The stripes are knitted in exactly the same way throughout the garment, but the end result of working in one piece is that the stripes on the sleeves go around the arm and on the body they run from top to bottom.

Working with two different yarns at the same time not only creates a thicker garment with a good drape—it also leads to interesting color effects within the stripes, which are created as you work.

When you are working on a project, always keep only the needles you are working with in your knitting bag, so you do not pick up and start using the wrong needles by mistake.

As you work, try to keep the stitches up towards the tip of the needles, so you do not stretch them out of shape as you work and spoil your gauge.

Heirloom Wrap

Kate Buchanan has created a fabulous addition to any wardrobe. Knitted in a luxurious mohair/silk blend, this ultra-soft and easy-to-make wrap looks stunning against a little black dress. Deceptively easy to make, create squares in two different stitch patterns and join them.

Materials

Yarn

Kidsilk Spray by Rowan, 1oz/25g ball, each approx 230 yd/210 m (70% mohair, 30% silk)
12 balls in Vino 576

Needles and extras

1 pair US 6 (4 mm) needles
US 6 (4 mm) circular needle
Sewing thread and needle
34 x 34 in. (85 × 85 cm) piece of lining fabric in a contrasting color (optional).

Gauge

20 sts and 25 rows to 4 in. (10 cm) over stocking stitch, on US 6 (4 mm) needles after blocking.

Special Abbreviations

tbl = insert right-hand needle into the back of the loop on the left-hand needle

Sizes and Measurements

Actual measurements: long side 33 in. (82.5 cm); **each square** 11 x 11in (27.5 x 27.5 cm)

Simple Lace Square (make 4)

Cast on 56 sts.
Work St st until work measures 2 in. (5 cm) from cast on edge, ending on a WS row.

Work Simple Lace panel:

Row 1 (RS): K1 *yo, k2tog; rep from * to last st, k1.
Row 2 and every alt row: Purl.
Row 3: K2 *yo, k2tog; rep from * to last 2, k2.
Row 5: K1 *yo, k2tog; rep from * to last st, k1.
Row 6: Purl.
Work St st for 2 in. (5cm).
Work 6 rows of Simple Lace pattern as above.
Work St st for 2 in. (5cm).
Work 6 rows of Simple Lace pattern as above.
Work St st for 2 in. (5cm).
Cast off.

Feather Lace Square (make 2)

Cast on 55 sts.
Work St st for 1¼ in. (3 cm), ending on a WS row.
Work Feather Lace panel as follows:
Row 1 (RS): K1 *yo, k2tog tbl, k1, k2tog, yo, k1; rep from * to end.
Row 2 and alt rows: Purl.

Row 3: K1 *yo, k1, sl1, k2tog, psso, k1, yo, k1; rep from * to end.

Row 5: K1 *k2tog, yo, k1, yo, k2tog tbl, k1; rep from * to end.

Row 7: k2tog *[k1, yo] twice, k1, sl 1, k2tog, psso; rep from * to last 5 sts,

[k1, yo] twice, k1, k2tog tbl.

Row 8: Purl.

Repeat this panel of 8 rows twice more.

Work 1¼ in. (3 cm) St st.

Work Feather Lace panel.
Work 1¼ in. (3 cm) St st.
Bind off.

Finishing

Press squares according to yarn label.
Lay out squares alternating Simple Lace and Feather Lace squares, with Simple Lace squares at each corner. Turn all Simple Lace squares 90° so that they are at lying at right angles to the Feather Lace squares. Sew together strips of squares. Then sew strips together.

Work picot point bind off:
Using a circular needle, pick up 138 sts along one long edge.
Work 3 rows St st.
Bind off 2 sts, *transfer st from right needle to left needle, cast on 2 sts, bind off 4 sts; rep from * until all sts have been bound off.
Pick up and work sts along the other long edge.
Weave in ends.

Optional lining:
Lay wrap on lining fabric and cut fabric to fit, allowing a ½ in. (12 mm) hem around each edge. Fold over ½ in. (12 mm) hem and press. Using herringbone stitch along edges, join lining fabric to throw carefully. Secure knitted fabric to lining with a few tiny sewn stitches at the cross point where four corners come together.

That's a Wrap

This project is not knitted in the round, but the circular needle allows enough room to pick up enough stitches along the entire edge when you knit the picot point bind off edging.

You can knit the squares on a circular needle as well if you prefer, but be careful not to stretch them out of shape as you work.

These squares can also be used to make a lovely lacy throw. Make 18 Simple Lace Squares and 17 Feather Lace Squares and lay them out in a checkerboard pattern, five by seven squares, with a Simple Lace Square in each corner. After sewing the squares together, make the picot point edging by picking up 230 stitches along the short edge and 322 on the long edge and work the edging as given in the pattern.

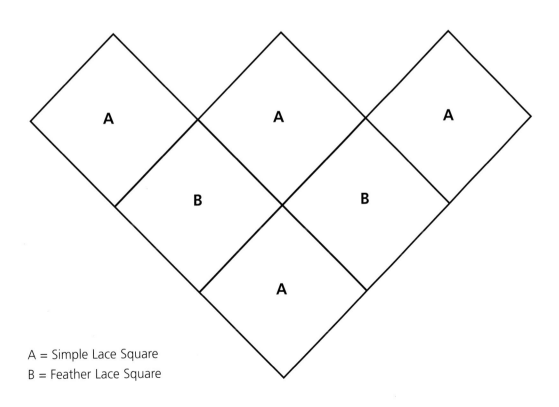

A = Simple Lace Square
B = Feather Lace Square

Accessories

Why sacrifice style for comfort? Whether it's a
Ladder-Stitch Neckwarmer or a Reversible Fair Isle Carryall,
these stylish accessories require little investment of time and
make ideal weekend projects. Your biggest hurdle will be
deciding which to knit first!

Ladder-Stitch Neckwarmer

With an incredibly soft and luxurious hand, Sîan Luyken's chic neckwarmer is a dream to knit in an alpaca/silk blend. The design requires only two balls of yarn, making it a quick-knit in easy stockinette. Suitable for the beginner who wants a challenge, this project utilizes grafting and provisional cast on— handy short cuts used in many patterns to give a seamless finish.

Materials

Yarn
Alpaca Silk by Debbie Bliss, 1¾oz/50g ball, each
    approx 114 yd/105 m (80% alpaca, 20% silk)
2 balls in 07

Needles and extras
1 pair US 10 (6 mm) needles
Yarn needle

Gauge
14 sts and 9 rows to 4 in. (10 cm) over St st,
    on US 10 (6 mm) needles. Take the time to check
    your gauge.

Special Abbreviations
W2 = insert right hand needle into next stitch as if
    to knit. Wrap the yarn twice around the needle
    and finish the stitch as normal.

W3 = wrap the yarn three times around the needle
    before finishing the stitch.

W4 = wrap the yarn four times around the needle
    before finishing the stitch.

When you come to purl these stitches, insert the
    right hand needle into the bottom of the stitch
    and purl as normal, allowing the wraps to fall.
    You will have created an extra long stitch. Be
    careful not to purl the wraps; if you're unsure of
    the technique then check that you still have the
    correct amount of stitches when you have finished
    purling the row.

Provisional Cast on

Hold a pair of knitting needles together. Make a slip knot with your working yarn and slip it over both needles. Hold the needles and one end of the waste yarn in your right hand, with the waste yarn running underneath the needles. Hold the working yarn and the rest of the waste yarn in your left hand. Pass the working yarn around the waste yarn counter-clockwise. Then bring it up to the left side of the needles and pass it around the needles clockwise. Pass the working yarn counter-clockwise around your waste yarn again and then clockwise around the needles to make your third stitch. Continue until you have cast on the required amount of stitches. Slip one needle out of the stitches and then start knitting as normal.

Kitchener stitch

Place the stitches from your provisional cast on edge on a knitting needle, removing the waste yarn. Hold this needle and your working needle beside each other so that the RS of your neckwarmer faces outwards. Cut the working yarn from the ball, leaving a tail approximately three times as long as your knitting edge. Thread this onto a blunt darning needle. Insert the darning needle purlwise through the first stitch of the needle closest to you (needle A) and pull the yarn through, leaving the stitch on needle A. Pass the yarn knitwise through the first stitch of the needle furthest away from you (needle B), leaving it on needle B. This has set you up to graft the two ends together.

Now insert the darning needle through the first stitch of needle A knitwise and slip it off the needle, pulling the yarn through. Insert the needle purlwise through the next stitch and leave it on needle A. Insert the needle purlwise through the first stitch of needle B, slip it off and pull the yarn through. Insert the darning needle knitwise through the next stitch and leave it on needle B. Repeat this process until you have one stitch left on each needle. Insert the darning needle knitwise into the stitch on needle A and take it off, then take the last stitch of needle B purlwise.

Use the darning needle to tidy up your grafting stitches; pull gently on each stitch from the end you started on to the end you finished on until they are the same tension as your knitted stitches. An invisible join!

Size

One size fits all.

Neckwarmer

Using the provisional cast on method, cast on 47 sts.
Row 1: Knit.
Row 2: Purl.
Row 3: K6, [W2, W3, W4, W3, W2, K5] four times, k1.
Row 4: Purl.
Row 5: Knit.
Row 6: Purl.
Row 7: K11 [W2, W3, W4, W3, W2, K5] three times, k6.
Row 8: Purl.
Row 9: Knit.
Row 10: Purl.
Rows 3–10 form the pattern. Repeat these rows 9 times more. (82 rows since cast-on)
Work first 5 rows of pattern.

Finishing

Join the two ends of your neckwarmer using Kitchener stitch.
Block firmly to stiffen up the ladder decoration.

Blue Note Hat & Scarf

This dapper stockinette-stitched hat-and-scarf set by Sîan Luyken keeps you looking your best all season long. The hat features a unique box top design, while the scarf is short and dense so it can be knotted neatly. You can create variations of this pattern by creating stripes or stitching in seed stitch. Be prepared to experiment!

Materials

Yarn
Nordic by Katia, 3½oz/100g skein, each approx
   55 yd/50 m (100% wool)
4 skeins in Denim Blue (A)
1 skein in White (B)

Needles and extras
1 or 2 × US 17 (12 mm) circular needles (see Note)
Large crochet hook
Length of stitching elastic

Gauge
9 sts and 12 rows to 4 in. (10 cm) over stockinette
   stitch, on US 17 (12 mm) needles. Gauge is not
   critical on this project, but if your gauge is very
   different change needle size to correct.

Special Abbreviations
M1 = slip the tip of the right-hand needles into the
   stitch directly below the first stitch of the left hand
   needle. Gently lift this stitch onto the left-hand
   needle and knit it.

Size
One size fits all.

Note
The cord of the circular needle is too wide for this
hat once you start working in the round, but if you
have two circular needles then you can place half
the stitches on one needle and half on the other.
If you only use one needle, avoid stretching the
fabric by pulling a loop of the excess cord between
two stitches so that some of the cord hangs loose
and all the stitches sit comfortably on the needle.

Hat

Cast on 4 stitches in A.

Row 1: Purl.

Row 2: K1, M1, k1, M1, k1, M1, k1: 7 sts.

Row 3: Purl.

Row 4: K1, *M1, k1* to end: 13 sts.

Row 5: Purl.

Row 6: K1 *M1, K1* to end: 25 sts.

Row 7: Purl.

Row 8: K1 *M1, K1* to end: 49 sts.

Row 9: Purl.

Row 10: Knit.

Join the work to form the sides of the hat as follows: Using two circular needles (see Note), slip a stitch marker or loop of waste yarn onto the right needle to mark where each row ends. Purl the next st and start working in a spiral, continuing to share the sts between the two needles. As you work around, keep re-pulling the cord and shifting the sts along.

Purl the next 4 rows.

Knit the next 4 rows.

Next row: K36 sts, yf, sl next st onto right needle and turn, yf. Sl st back onto right needle. This forms beg of short row.

Next row: P23 sts, yb, sl next st onto right needle and turn, yb. Sl st back onto right needle.

Continue working back and forth, dec short row by 1 st at either end.

Work 6 rows.

Next round: K to end of short row. Pick up wrap of next st and sl onto left needle. Knit wrap together with the next st. Continue round until all the wraps have been picked up, k to the end of round.

Next round: Change to B, work 3 rounds.

Bind off.

Scarf

Row 1: Using A, cast on 24 sts.

Row 2: Sl 1, k to end.

Row 3: Sl 1, p to end.

Continue working in St st, slipping first st of every row, until you have used three skeins of A.

Bind off.

Finishing

Sew up the crown seam of hat and weave in the ends. Block to shape. If the hat is loose, thread a length of shirring elastic through the brim.

Weave in the ends of the scarf and press.

Making fringe

Cut 96 lengths of B, each measuring 6 in. (15 cm). Using a large crochet hook, pull pairs of threads through between the cast-on and bound-off sts and knot. Use 24 knots at either end to form the fringe.

Warm Thoughts

This hat-and-scarf set looks really clever, but the denim color of the yarn means it also looks great worn casually with jeans. The design suits both men and women, so you could knit two sets!

The Katia yarn is really easy to knit and is very soft— this hat and scarf will be suitable for even the most delicate skin!

When you are not working on it, keep your work in a fabric bag to keep everything together and to keep the yarn clean. Fabric is better than plastic, as it is easy for the needles to tear holes in the plastic—allowing small items to fall out.

Reversible Fair Isle Carryall

This carefree tote designed by Kate Buchanan can be flipped inside out to reveal a darker more sophisticated version for the evening. Don't let this pattern deceive you: it might appear complex, but it's essentially knitting and purling with two different colored strands of yarn. Once you get the hang of this technique, known as Fair Isle, you'll be Double Knitting like a pro!

Materials

Yarn

Aran by GiftedKnits, 1¾oz/50g skein, each
   approx 92 yd/85 m (100% wool)
2 skeins in Crystal (A)
2 skeins in Jade (B)

Needles and extras

1 pair US 8 (5 mm) needles
2 × 1 in. (2.5 cm) buttons
Yarn needle

Gauge

16 sts and 20 rows to 4 in. (10 cm) using special
   Double Knitting technique without motif, on US 8
   (5 mm) needles. Gauge is not important but
   technique will give a looser gauge than normal.

Note

To practice the Double Knitting technique, cast on
   10 pairs of stitches and repeat rows 1 and 2 of
   the pattern for a few rows.

Special Abbreviations

YF = bring both colors forward between the needles
YB = pull both colors back between needles
K1A = Knit 1 st of color A

Sizes and Measurements

Actual measurements: width 8¾ in. (22 cm); **length** 7¼ in. (18 cm); **length of strap** 17½ in. (44 cm)

Double Knitting

The technique of double knitting produces a thick, reversible fabric and it is really quite simple to learn. Basically, you knit one side and purl the other side at the same time, so you are actually knitting two pieces of fabric at once. The best way to understand it is to make a sample square, which you can easily make into a handy potholder afterwards!

Using two different colors together cast on 15 pairs of stitches (15 of one color and 15 of the other). This gives a tight solid edge that is perfect for bag making. Make sure you always knit one color, while purling the other. Start by knitting 1 stitch of color A, then bring both colors of yarn forward in between the two needles. Now purl color B and pull both colors back between the needles. Keep knitting with color A and purling with color B, remembering to bring BOTH colors forward and back each time to the end of the row.

Always twist the two colors together at the beginning of the row before you start knitting to prevent the two pieces separating untidily at the edges. It's important to knit the color that is facing you, while purling the color that is on the other side, so that you get a smooth stockinette stitch surface on both sides.

There is also a knack to joining in new yarn. Try to join a new strand of yarn at the beginning of a row as follows: Make a slip knot in the new yarn and slide it onto the tail of the old strand. Then bring the loose ends forward and back with the main two strands for 10 stitches. You can then trim the ends when you've finished knitting.

Note

You can actually use this technique to knit two socks at the same time, one inside the other. This is because the two pieces of fabric are knitted separately but at the same time.

Bag

Using the two colors together, cast on 35 PAIRS of stitches so you have 35 stitches in A and 35 in B. Work double knitting technique as follows:

Row 1: *K1A, YF, P1B, YB; rep from * to end of row.
Row 2: *K1B, YF, P1A, YB; rep from * to end of row.
Repeat Rows 1 and 2 until you have 24 rows from the cast on edge.

Motif pattern:

Note Always remember to bring YF before a purl st and YB before a knit st.
Row 1: *K1A, P1B, K1A, P1B, K1B, P1A, K1A, P1B, K1A, P1B; rep from * to end of row.
Row 2: *K1B, P1A, K1A, P1B, K1A, P1B, K1A, P1B, K1B, P1A; rep from * to end of row
Row 3: As Row 1.
Now work 3 rows of plain Double Knitting.
These 6 rows form the Motif Pattern on the bag.
Repeat these 6 rows two more times until you have 42 rows from the cast on edge. You should have 3 rows of motifs.

Make fold at bottom of bag:

With A facing you, *P1A, YB, K1B, YF; rep from * to end of row.
With B facing you, *P1B, YB, K1A, YF; rep from * to end of row.
Work 3 rows of plain Double Knitting.
Work 3 rows of Motif Pattern.
Repeat these 6 rows two more times so you have 18 rows from the fold rows.
Work 18 rows of plain Double Knitting.

Make buttonhole:

Row 1: With A facing you, K1A, YF, P1B, YB for 32 sts then bind off 3 PAIRS of sts as follows: [k2tog, k2tog, pass right pair of sts over left pair, k2tog, pass right pair over left, k2tog, pass right pair over left], K1A, YF, P1B, YB to the end of row.

Row 2: With B facing you, K1B, YF, P1A, YB for 30 sts then slip 1 pair of sts. Turn work around. Cast on 2 pair of sts, YF, Slip 1 pair, YB, cast on 1 pair. Turn work back so B is facing you. K1B, YF, P1A, YB to the end of row.

Work 4 rows of plain Double Knitting.

With A facing you, bind off pairs of sts.

Strap

With both strands together, cast on 1 pair of sts.
K1A, YF, P1B, turn.
Cast on 1 pair of sts, K1B, YF, P1A.
Repeat until you have 5 pairs of sts; 10 sts.
Starting with K1A, work 40 rows of plain Double Knitting.
Work the 3 row Motif Pattern as follows:

Row 1: *K1A, P1B, K1A, P1B, K1B, P1A, K1A, P1B, K1A, P1B.

Row 2: *K1B, P1A, K1A, P1B, K1A, P1B, K1A, P1B, K1B, P1A.

Row 3: as Row 1.

Work 6 rows of plain Double Knitting.
Repeat these 9 rows until you have 9 motifs.
After the 9th motif, work 40 rows of plain Double Knitting. Check your 40 rows line up with the 40 rows on other side before starting to decrease.
Bind off 1 pair of sts at beginning of every row until there are none left.

Making up

Press both sides of each piece firmly. The ends of the strap form the gussets on the sides of the bag. Use 80 in. (200 cm) of B to sew up each side of your bag.

Lay bag and strap down with B side up. Line up the tip of the strap end with the fold row and starting at the fold row, join the two B edges using mattress stitch. When you have reached the top of the bag part, switch to blanket stitch and sew along the edge of the strap until you get to the point where you need to join the other side of the bag onto the strap. Use mattress stitch to join the bag edge to the strap all the way down to the fold rows. You may need more yarn at this stage. Do exactly the same mattress stitch up the other side of the bag, blanket stitch along the edge of the strap and mattress stitch down the final side.

Finally, stitch one button to the back of the bag, opposite the buttonhole on the front, then sew the other button on the reverse side of the back in the same position. You can even sew them on at the same time!

Whimsical Winter Warmers

Laura Long's spirited pompom-accented accessories make winter dressing fun!
Both the decorative mittens and matching hat boast a fetching all-over diamond pattern,
while the scarf speaks volumes with its lighthearted motif and pompom fringes.

Materials

Yarn

Wool Cotton by Rowan, 1¾oz/50g ball, each approx
123 yd/113 m (50% wool, 50% cotton)

3 balls in Laurel 960 (A)

3 balls in Aloof 958 (B)

3 balls in Citron 901 (C)

3 balls in Hiss 952 (D)

Needles and extras

Circular US 10 (6 mm) needles

Pair US 10 (6 mm) needles

Yarn needle

Pompom maker or two circles of cardboard each
2 in. (5 cm) in diameter and with a ¾ in. (18 mm)
diameter central hole.

Gauge

17 sts and 24 rows to 4 in. (10 cm) over
stockinette stitch, on US 10 (6 mm) needles,
using two ends of yarn. If your gauge is
drastically off, change your needle size to achieve
the correct gauge. However, it doesn't matter at
what gauge the scarf is knitted.

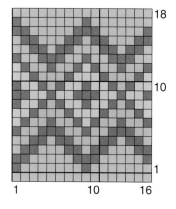

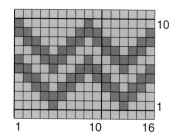

Zigzag pattern 1

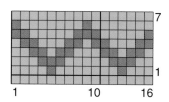

Zigzag pattern 2

Sizes
Mitten, hat and scarf: One size fits all.

Left Mitten
With circular needles cast on 32 sts in A.
Knit 3 rounds in A.
Knit 1 round in B.
Begin to work diamond pattern, following the chart.
Work 17 rounds from chart.
Cont in B only.

Shape left thumb gusset:
Round 1: K11, p1, [inc 1 st in next st] 2 times, k1, p1, k to end.
Round 2: K11, p1, k5, p1, k to end.
Round 3: K11, p1, k5, p1, k to end.
Round 4: K11, p1, k5, p1, k to end.
Round 5: K11, p1, inc 1 st in next st, k2 until 2 sts

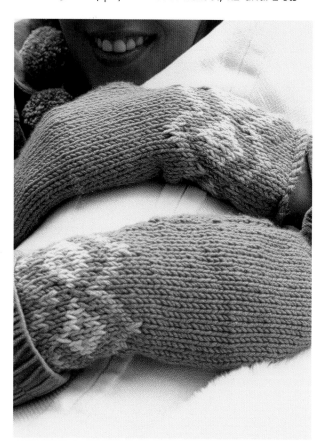

before p st, inc 1 st in next st, k1, p1, k to end.
Continue as above, inc every fourth row until there are 11 sts between the 2 purl sts.
Work 3 rows as set.

Shape left thumb using straight needles:
Row 1: K23 sts, turn.
Row 2: Inc 1 st, p10, turn.
Row 3: Cast on 1 st, k12, turn: 13 sts.
Continue on these 13 sts for 11 rows.
Next row: *K1, k2tog; repeat from * to last st, k1.
Cut yarn and draw up sts.
Stitch thumb seam.

Make hand:
Pick up 5 sts at the base on thumb on circular needles.
Arrange sts and go back to starting st. (34 sts)
Knit for 16 rows.

Shape top:
Row 1: K1, sl 1, k1, psso, k11, k2tog, k2, sl 1, k1, psso, k11, k2tog, k1.
Row 2: and every alt row: Knit.
Row 3: K1, sl 1, k1, psso, k9, k2tog, k2, sl 1, k1, psso, k9, k2tog, k1.
Repeat rows 2 and 3 having 2 less sts between decreasing until 14 sts remain.
Split sts onto 2 needles, bind off in pairs inside out.

Right Mitten
Work as for left mitten until thumb gusset.

Shape right thumb gusset:
Round 1: K16, p1, k1, [inc 1 st in next st] 2 times, p1, k to end of row.
Continue with increases as for left mitten.

Shape right thumb
Row 1: K16, p1, k11, turn.

Change to straight needles.

Row 2: Inc 1 st, p10, turn.

Row 3: Cast on 1 st, k12, turn; 13 sts.

Cont thumb and rest of right mitten as for left mitten.

Finishing

Sew in ends on wrong side of work.

Hat

With circular needles cast on 80 sts in A

Knit 5 rounds in A.

Knit 6 rounds in B.

Work one diamond pattern, following the chart, for 17 rounds.

Knit 4 rounds in B.

Start zigzag pattern 2, following the chart for 6 rounds.

Change to B and knit 2 rounds.

Shape top:

Row 1: K3, *k2tog, k6; repeat from * until last 5 sts, k2tog, k3; 70 sts.

Knit 6 rounds.

Next round: K3, * k2tog, k5; repeat from * until last 4 sts, k2tog, k2; 60 sts.

Knit 6 rounds.

Next round: K3, *k2tog, k4; repeat from * until last 3 sts, k2tog, k1; 50 sts.

Knit 6 rounds.

Next round: * k2tog, k3; repeat from * to end.

Knit 5 rounds.

Change to D.

Knit 1 round.

Next round: * k2tog, k2; repeat from * to end.

Change to B.

Knit 2 rounds.

Change to A

Knit 2 rounds.

Change to B.

Knit 2 rounds.

Next round: * k2tog, k1; repeat from * to end.

Knit 6 rounds.

Next round: K2tog to end of row; 10 sts.

Knit 2 rounds.

Take sts off needle and pass thread through sts. leaving slightly open. This is where you will put the pompom braids.

Making braids

Cut three lengths of yarn in B and knot at one end. Braid the yarn then knot the other end. Make 3 braids, each different lengths.

Making pompoms

Make three pompoms in A, C and D, using the pom pom maker. If you are using circles of cardboard, place the two circles together then wind lengths of yarn around and through the central hole until it is full. Cut the yarn between the two pieces of card, but before pulling them off completely tie a piece of yarn tightly in the gap to hold the pompom together.

Finishing

Attach one pompom to the end of each braid.
Tie the 3 braids together and thread inside the hole at the top of the hat. The pompoms should hang down the sides of the hat. Pull the yarn around the hole tightly to close it and hold the pompoms in place.

Scarf

Cast on 32 sts with waste yarn and knit a few rows.
Change to A and proceed in St st as follows:

Row 1: Knit.

Row 2: Purl.

These two rows form St st pattern. Continue in pattern, changing yarn color and working chart design as indicated.

Change to B and work 2 rows.
Change to A and work 2 rows.
Change to B and work 2 rows.
Change to A and work 2 rows.
Change to B and work 8 rows.
Change to D and work 2 rows.
Change to B and work 2 rows.
Change to D and work 2 rows.
Change to B and work 14 rows.
Work one zigzag pattern 1 across scarf, following 16 sts of chart twice and using B and D.
Change to B and work 10 rows.
*Change to A and work 2 rows.
Change to B and work 2 rows.
Change to C and work 2 rows.
Change to B and work 2 rows.
Change to D and work 2 rows.
Change to B and work 2 rows.
Change to C and work 2 rows.
Change to B and work 2 rows.
Change to A and work 2 rows.**
Change to B and work 24 rows.
Work one zigzag pattern 1 across scarf, following chart and using B and D.

Change to B and work 24 rows.
Repeat from * to **.
Change to B and work 16 rows.
***Change to D and work 2 rows.
Change to B and work 2 rows.
Change to A and work 2 rows.
Change to C and work 2 rows.
Change to D and work 2 rows.
Change to C and work 2 rows.
Change to A and work 2 rows.
Change to B and work 2 rows.
Change to D and work 2 rows.
Change to B and work 2 rows. ****
Repeat from *** to **** 5 times.
Work a further 6 rows in St st.
Change to A and work 2 rows.
Change to B and work 2 rows.
Change to A and work 2 rows.
Change to B and work 2 rows.
Change to A and work 2 rows.

Make three triangle points:

Triangle 1

Working on only first 11sts with A, work with RS (knit) facing.

Row 1: Knit

Row 2 and every alt row: Purl.

Row 3: K2, k2tog, k3, k2tog, k2.

Row 5: Knit.

Row 7: K2, k2tog, k1, k2tog, k2.

Row 9: Knit.

Row 11: K2, k2tog, k2tog, k1.

Row 13: Knit.

Row 15: K2, k2tog, k1.

Row 17: K1, k2tog, k1.

Row 19: K3tog.

Cut yarn and pull through the last st.

Triangle 2

Attach yarn again, and using only the center 10 sts, work with RS (knit) facing.

Row 1: Knit.

Row 2 and every alt row: Purl.

Row 3: K2, k2tog, k2, k2tog, k2.

Row 5: Knit.

Row 7: K2, k2tog, k2tog, k2.

Row 9: Knit.

Row 11: K1, k2tog, k2tog, k1.

Row 13: Knit

Row 15: K1, k2tog, k1.

Row 17: K3tog

Cut yarn and pull through the last st.

Triangle 3

Work as for Triangle 1, using the last 11 sts and working with RS (knit) facing.

Unravel waste yarn at beginning of scarf and complete three triangle points with A at this end as already described.

Making braids

Cut three lengths of yarn in different colors, each approx 16 in. (40 cm) and knot at one end. Braid the yarn then knot the other end. Make 6 braids, each around 12 in. (30 cm) long.

Making pompoms

Make 12 pompoms, some in each color, using the pompom maker. If you are using circles of cardboard, place the two circles together then wind lengths of yarn around and through the central hole until it is full. Cut the yarn between the pieces of cardboard, but before pulling apart completely tie a piece of yarn tightly in the gap to hold the pompom together.

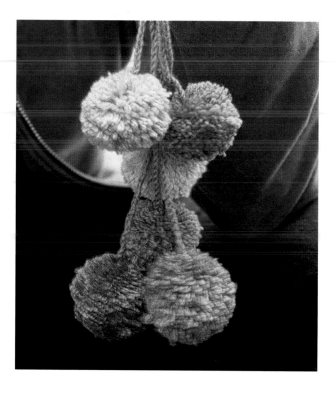

Finishing

Attach one pompom to each end of each braid. Join the center of one braid to the bottom end of each triangle so that the pompoms hang down.

Casting Call

Casting on with the waste yarn and then pulling it out means that there is no cast-on edge, so you can go back again and work the points at the beginning without there being an obvious join.

If you are interrupted while working, or cannot finish a project in one sitting, always finish your row before you put your work down. If you leave it with the needles in halfway, these stitches will stretch and the texture of the fabric may well remain uneven at this point.

Washing a finished item can often sort out minor unevenness in the fabric.

Pod Pocket Cozy

Pump up the volume! This MP3 player case, designed by Kate Buchanan, is in the style of denim jeans with a handle, pocket for headphones, and contrasting yellow stitching. The main body is simple knit stitch in one long strip, with a shaped seed-stitched flap at one end.

Materials

Yarn
Washed Haze DK by Patons, 1¾oz/50g ball, each
    approx 130 yd/120 m (50% cotton, 50% acrylic)
1 ball in Denim 00004

Needles and extras
1 pair US 3 (3.25 mm) needles
1 pair of hook-and-loop pads
Yarn needle
1 skein of yellow embroidery floss or thick sewing
    cotton (optional)
Sewing needle (optional)

Gauge
24 sts and 32 rows to 4 in. (10 cm) over
    stockinette stitch, on US 3 (3.25 mm) needles. If
    necessary change needle size to obtain this
    gauge.

Special Abbreviations
Sppo = Slip 1, p1, pass slipped st over.
P2tog = Purl 2 together.

Sizes and Measurements
Actual measurements: Overall size 4½ × 3 in. (11 × 7.5 cm)

Main Body
Cast on 21 sts.
Row 1: * K1, p1; rep from * to last st, k1.
Repeat this row twice more.
Starting with a k row, work St st until work measures 9¼ in. (23 cm) from cast on edge, ending on a RS row.

Shape flap:
Row 1: With WS facing, Sppo, p to last 2 sts, p2tog.
Row 2: Skpo, k to last 2 sts, k2tog: 17 sts.
Row 3: Purl.
Row 4: K8, yo, k2tog, k7.
(this puts in a hole for the headphone jack)
Row 5: Purl.
Row 6: Knit.
Row 7: Purl.
Row 8: K2tog, *k1, p1; rep from * to last st, k1.
Row 9: K2tog, *k1, p1; rep from * to end.
Row 10: P2tog, *p1, k1; rep from * to last st, p1.
Row 11: P2tog, *p1, k1; rep from * to end.
Repeat rows 8–11, then rows 8–9: 7 sts.
Bind off 7 sts.

Pocket

Cast on 23 sts.

Continue in St st until work measures 2¾ in. (7 cm).

With RS facing, bind off 13sts, k to end. (10 sts)

Next row: Purl.

Next row: Skpo, k to end.

Repeat last 2 rows until there are 4 sts remaining.

Continue in St st until work measures 4½ in. (11.5 cm) from cast on edge.

Bind off.

Work edging:

Starting on right-hand side, pick up 13 sts along RS top edge then 7 sts up the sloping edge: 20 sts.

Knit one row.

Bind off 20 sts.

Handle

Cast on 40 sts.

Knit into the back of every st. (This stops your work from curling.)

Next row: Knit.

Next row: Knit.

Bind off purlwise.

Finishing

Fold body piece so that cast on edge matches dec rows at start of flap. Lay pocket on the side with flap and join side seams, trapping pocket sides at the same time. Overstitch bottom edge of pocket along fold line.

Join ends of handle to one or both of the side seams. Attach matching hook-and-loop pads to flap and front of main body.

Optional

Using running stitch, stitch a pattern as shown in the photograph onto the front side (the side without the flap), and along the edging of the pocket. Finish by going back along the line with running stitch to complete the lines.

Pocket Play

The Pod Pocket in our picture has been deliberately styled to look like a pair of denim jeans, but it is easy to make something very different just by omitting the stitching and using a brighter color yarn. Try making it in bright pink, with an embroidered heart, for the little princess in your life!

No MP3 player? Make the Pocket anyway and use it to carry a cell phone instead! If you don't need to use your phone in handsfree mode with a headset, you can omit the eyelet hole for the jack plug.

Always try to knit in a good light so there is less strain on your eyes as you work.

Cable-Tasseled Scarf

*This sumptuous cable scarf by Louise Butt is knit with super chunky yarn
to ensure that you stay ultra-warm when temperatures drop. The scarf
is designed so that the tassels are a part of the cable pattern, which
then seamlessly continues into the main body.*

Materials

Yarn

Bigga by Sirdar, 3½oz/100g ball, each approx
44 yd/40 m (50% wool, 50% acrylic)
6 balls in Chamois 686

Needles and extras

1 pair of US 19 (15 mm) needles
1 stitch holder
1 kinked cable needle
Yarn needle

Gauge

6 sts and 9 rows to 4 in. (10 cm) over stockinette
stitch, on US 19 (15 mm) needles. If necessary
change needle size to obtain this gauge.

Special Abbreviations

C6B = Place first 3 sts on cable needle and hold at
back of work, k next 3 sts, then k3 sts from
cable needle.

Size

Actual measurements: length 51 in. (130 cm)
excluding tassels.

Tassels (Make 3)

Cast on 6 sts using US 19 (15 mm) needles.
Row 1: Knit.
Row 2: Purl.
Row 3: Knit.
Row 4: Purl.
Row 5: C6B.
Row 6: Purl.
Rep last 6 rows twice more.
Next row: Knit.
Next row: Purl.
Place sts on a stitch holder.

Join tassels for body of scarf as follows:
Joining row: K6 sts of first tassel from stitch holder,
turn, cast on 3 sts, turn, k6 sts of next tassel, turn,
cast on 3 sts, turn, k6 sts of last tassel: 24 sts.
Next row: [P6, k3] twice, p6.
Next row: [C6B, p3] twice, C6B.
Next row: [P6, k3] twice, p6.
Next row: *[K6, p3] twice, k6.
Next row: [P6, k3] twice, p6.
Next row: [K6, p3] twice, k6.
Next row: [P6, k3] twice, p6.
Next row: [C6B, p3] twice, C6B.

Next row: P6.
Next row: Knit.
Next row: Purl.
Next row: Knit.*****
Next row: Purl.****
Rep from *** to **** once more, then from *** to *****.
Bind off these 6 sts purlwise.

Rejoin yarn, bind off 3 sts purlwise, knit until 6 sts rem on right needle, turn.
Next row: P6.
Work tassel from *** in the same way, then rep for final tassel.

Finishing

Sew in all ends. Pin tassels to a heatproof board so that the cable pattern is face up. Hold a steaming iron just above the tassels for a few seconds then leave to dry thoroughly.

Long Haul...

It may sound great if a friend offers to help you knit something—particularly if she is a good knitter—but beware! Different knitters will work to a slightly different gauge, so the sections she does may well look different to your own.

This yarn is quite chunky and the needles used are quite large. Make sure your cable needle is long enough to hold the stitches you need to carry, without them slipping off too easily.

Cables pull the fabric in—just like ribbing does—so the gauge will be much tighter than for a flat fabric. Pattern instructions that include cables will always allow for this.

Next row: [P6, k3] twice, p6. **
Rep from * until body of scarf measures approx 51 in. (130 cm), ending on ** row.
Next row: [K6, p3] twice, k6.
Next row: [P6, k3] twice, p6.

Split for tassels:
Next row: K6 turn, and work on just these sts.
Next row: P6.
Next row: ***C6B.

Textured Hat & Scarf

*Laura Long's short textured scarf fits perfectly around your neck
to keep it toasty warm without the extra length of a conventional scarf; the
complementary hat makes for cool comfort. The textured pattern combined
with the blending of two different yarns creates added visual interest.*

Materials

Yarn
Matchmaker Merino 4 ply by Jaeger,
 1¾oz/50g ball, each approx 200 yd/183 m
 (100% merino wool)
2 balls in Lilac 742 (A)
Baby Merino DK by Jaeger, 1¾oz/50g ball, each
 approx 131 yd/120 m (100% merino wool)
2 balls in Hula Hoop 194 (B)

Needles and extras
Pair US 3 (3.25 mm) needles
Yarn needle
1 large button

Gauge
8 sts and 12 rows to 4 in. (10 cm) over stockinette
 stitch, on US 3 (3.25 mm) needles, using 2
 strands of A and 1 strand of B.

Size
Actual measurements: scarf length 31½ in.
(80 cm); **hat** one size fits all.

Scarf
Cast on 26 sts.
Work k2, p2 rib for 6 rows.

Start textured pattern:
Row 1: Purl.
Row 2: K1, *(k1, p1, k1) into next st, p3tog; rep
from * to last st, k1.
Row 3: Purl.
Row 4: K1, *p3tog, (k1, p1, k1) into next st; rep
from * to last st, k1.
These four rows form pattern.
Repeat pattern 20 times more.

Make buttonhole:
Next row: P13, bind off 2 sts, p to end of row.
Next row: K1, *(k1, p1, k1) into next st, p3tog*, rep
from * to *, (k1, p1, k1) into next st, p1, cast on 2
sts, p1, p3tog, rep from * to * twice, k1.
Next row: Purl.
Next row: K1, *p3tog, (k1, p1, k1) into next st; rep
from * to last st, k1.

Repeat pattern rows 1–4 once more.
Purl one row.
Work k2, p2 rib for 6 rows.
Bind off.
Sew on button.

Hat

Cast on 50 sts.
Work k2, p2 rib for 6 rows.

Start textured pattern:

Row 1: Purl.
Row 2: K1, *(k1, p1, k1) into next st, p3tog; rep from * to last st, k1.
Row 3: Purl.
Row 4: K1, *p3tog, (k1 ,p1, k1) into next st; rep from * to last st, k1.
Repeat rows 1–4 four times more.

Start shaping:

Row 21: P10, p3tog, *p9, p3tog, repeat from * to last st, p1.
Row 22: As row 2.
Row 23: P2, p3tog *p5, p3tog, repeat from * to last 5 sts, p5.
Row 24: K1, *p3tog, (k1, p1, k1); rep from * to last 3 sts, p3tog.
Row 25: *P1, p3tog; rep from * to last 2 sts, p2.
Thread cut end of yarn through rem sts and pull tightly to close.

Finishing

Sew up the hat and weave in the ends.

Knit Wit

Using the two different yarns together creates a warm and chunky fabric, while the two toning colors give an interested mottled effect.

When choosing needles, check the points. Make sure they are not damaged in any way and are not too sharp, nor too blunt.

Needles not only come in different sizes, they also come in different lengths. Try to match the length to the number of stitches you are working with—trying to manage lots of stitches on a short needle can easily lead to dropped stitches, while working with very long needles on a tiny project is unwieldy.

Using yarns from different dye lots is not too much of an issue on this project, as a slight difference in color will probably be lost in the mottled effect. If you have no choice but to buy yarns across different dye lots for a project with plain knitting, try to use one dye lot for the main pieces and use up the odd balls for the ribbing or small separate pieces such as the collar.

Home Accents

Home is where the heart is—especially if it means creating a collection of fabulous pillows, throws, and more. Add a touch of glamour with the Foxy Cushion or try out the unusual Loopy Rug. Use this opportunity to explore your creative side and work with colors that compliment your decor.

Foxy Cushion

Designed by Louise Butt, this dramatic, yet simple-to-knit, cushion will be the talking point in any room! Drawing inspiration from the monochromatic style of the Sixties, this fabulous furry home accent is an updated design that will fit into most contemporary design schemes.

Materials

Yarn

(For one side of the cushion)
Foxy by Sirdar, 1¾oz/50g ball, each approx
    44 yd/40 m (100% polyester)
3 balls in Beaver 418 (A)
2 balls in Ermine 417 (B)

Needles and extras

A pair of US 10½ (7 mm) needles
24 × 24 in. (60 × 60 cm) piece of black suedette
    backing fabric
Sewing needle and yarn
22 × 22 in. (55 × 55 cm) pillow form

Gauge

12.5 sts and 17 rows to 4 in. (10 cm) over
    stockinette stitch, on US 10½ (7 mm) needles
Note that the nature of this yarn means the fabric
    will drop when finished, so check size of
    finished piece before cutting backing fabric.

Sizes and Measurements

Actual measurements: finished cushion 22⅜ × 22⅜ in. (56 × 56 cm)

Cushion front

Using US 10½ (7 mm) needles, cast on 20 sts in A, 20 sts in B, and 20 sts with A.
Keeping colors correct and remembering to strand the two yarns together on the reverse of the knitting when changing colors (see page 47), work 26 rows in St st so you have 3 blocks of color.
Next Row: Change colors, working B above A, A above B, and then B above A.
Work 24 rows in St st on this middle section.
Next Row: Change the colors again and work the final three blocks as the first for 26 rows.
Bind off.

Finishing

Cut the suedette fabric in half and hem along one long edge. Lay the two pieces RS upwards with the hemmed edges overlapping around 1 in. (2.5 cm). Lay the knitted piece on top, RS together and sew the knitted piece onto the backing. Turn RS out and insert the cushion pad through the slit. Alternatively, you can knit another square for the back—in which case you will need twice as much yarn.

Sudoku Blanket

The Japanese puzzle of Sudoku is taking the planet by storm. This design by Louise Butt converts the famous grid of three by three sets of nine squares, where numbers from 1-9 cannot be repeated in any set or row, into a pattern for a blanket. Colors replace the numbers, and to add texture there are nine different patterns to get your needles around.

Materials

Yarn

Bonus Chunky by Sirdar, 3½oz/100g ball, each
   approx 149 yd/137 m (100% Acrylic)

3 balls in Angel Pink 921 (A)

3 balls in Bluebell 969 (B)

3 balls in Denim 994 (C)

3 balls in Navy 971 (D)

3 balls in Maroon 918 (E)

3 balls in Fuchsia 990 (F)

3 balls in Signal Red 977 (G)

3 balls in Aran 933 (H)

3 balls in Violet 985 (I)

Needles and extras

1 pair of US 10½ (6.5 mm) needles

Yarn needle

Gauge

14 sts and 9 rows to 4 in. (10 cm) over stockinette
   stitch, on US 10½ (6.5 mm) needles. If necessary
   change needle size to obtain this gauge.

Special abbreviations

sl1 pwise = insert right-hand needle into next st as
   if to purl it, then slip it without working to right-
   hand needle

Hip to Be Square

A consistent gauge is really important on this project, as you need the 81 squares to be square and more or less the same size. However, as long as all your squares are almost equal, when sewn up they should all join together well.

For minor variations in square size, try a bit of blocking and pressing to stretch or shrink them down as described on pages 58–9.

Each of the nine patterns should be knitted once in each of the nine colors. When you have finished, you should have 81 different squares.

Do one pattern in all nine colors first because then you will be in the swing of the stitches.

This afghan does not have a border, but if you would like one, try one of the edgings on pages 166–7.

Sizes and Measurements
Actual measurements: 72 × 72 in.
(180 × 180 cm); **each motif** 8 in. (20 cm) square

Square 1 (Make one in each color yarn)
Cast on 44 sts.
Row 1 and every alt row: Purl.
Row 2: *K2tog tbl without sliding them off the left needle, now knit into the back of the first st again and slide both sts off the needle; rep from * to end of row.
Row 4: K1 tbl, *k2tog tbl without sliding them off the left needle, now k into the back of the first st again and slide both sts of the needle; rep from * to last st, k1 tbl.
Rep these 4 rows until work measures 8 in. (20 cm)
Bind off.

Square 2 (Make one in each color yarn)
Cast on 42 sts.
Row 1 and every alt row: Knit.
Row 2: P3, *[p1, k1, p1] into the next st, k3tog; rep from * to last 3 sts, p3.
Row 4: P3, *k3tog, [p1, k1, p1] into the nest stitch; rep from * to last 3 sts, p3.
Rep these 4 rows until work measures 8 in. (20 cm), ending on a row 3.
Next row: Purl.
Bind off.

Square 3 (Make one in each color yarn)
Cast on 33 sts.
Rows 1, 3, 5 and 7: Purl.
Rows 2, 4 and 6: K1, p1, *k4, p1: rep from * to last st, k1.
Row 8: Purl.
Rep these 8 rows until work measures 8 in. (20 cm)
Bind off.

Square 4 (Make one in each color yarn)
Cast on 40 sts.
Row 1: *With right-hand needle behind first st, knit second st tbl, k first st; rep from * to end.
Row 2: *P second st, p first st; rep from * to end.
Rep these 2 rows until work measures 8 in. (20 cm)
Bind off.

Square 5 (Make one in each color yarn)
Cast on 36 sts.
Row 1: *K1, yf, sl1 pwise, yb; rep from * to end.
Row 2 and every 4th row: Purl.
Row 3: *Yf, sl1 pwise, yb, k1; rep from * to end.
Rep these 4 rows until work measures 8 in. (20 cm)
Bind off.

Square 6 (Make one in each color yarn)
Cast on 42 sts.
Row 1: Knit.
Row 2: P1, (k2tog) to last st, p1.
Row 3: K1, *(k1, k1tbl) all into next st; rep from * to last st, k1.
Row 4: Purl.
Rep these 2 rows until work measures 8 in. (20 cm)
Bind off.

Square 7 (Make one in each color yarn)
Cast on 32 sts.
Row 1: Knit.
Row 2: Purl.
Row 3: K1, *k2tog, yo, k1, yo, sl1, k1, psso, k5; rep from * to last st, k1.
Row 4: P1, *p7, sl1, p2; rep from * to last st p1.
Row 5: As row 3.
Row 6: As row 4.
Row 7: Knit.
Row 8: Purl.
Row 9: K1, *k5, k2tog, yo, k1, yo, sl1, k1, psso; rep from * last st, k1.
Row 10: P1, *p2, sl1, p7; rep from * to last st, p1.

Row 11: As row 9.
Row 12: As row 10.
Rep these 12 rows until work measures 8 in. (20 cm) Bind off.

Square 8 (Make one in each color yarn)
Cast on 36 sts.
Row 1: * K3, p5, k3, p1; rep from * to end.
Row 2 and every alt row: Knit.
Row 3: P1, *k3, p3; rep from * to last 5 sts, k3, p2.
Row 5: P2, *k3, p1, k3, p5; rep from * to last 10 sts, k3, p1, k3, p3.
Row 7: *P3, k5, p3, k1; rep from * to end.
Row 9: K1, *p3, k3; rep from * to last 5 sts, p3, k2.
Row 11: K2, *p3, k1, p3, k5; rep from * to last 10 sts, p3, k1, p3, k3.
Row 12: As 2nd row.
Rep these 12 rows until work measures 8 in. (20 cm) Bind off.

Square 9 (Make one in each color yarn)
Cast on 36 sts.
Row 1: P2, *p3, [k1, yo, k1] into next st; rep from * to last 2 sts, p2.
Row 2: K2, *p3, k3; rep from * to last 2 sts, k2.
Row 3: P2, *p3, k3; rep from * to last 2 sts, p2.
Row 4: K2 *p3tog, k3; rep from * to last 2 sts, k2.
Row 5: Purl.
Row 6: Knit.
Row 7: P2, *p1, [k1, yo, k1] into next st, p2; rep from * to last 2 sts, p2.
Row 8: K4, *p3, k3; rep from * to end.
Row 9: P3, *k3, p3; rep from * to last 7 sts, k3, p4.
Row 10: K4, *p3tog, k3; rep from * to end.
Row 11: Purl.
Row 12: Knit.
Rep these 12 rows until work measures 8 in. (20 cm) Bind off.

Finishing
Hold a steam iron over the reverse of each square so that they are easier to sew together.
Lay all squares face up on a large flat surface, following the colors and patterns in the grid. Using a backstitch, sew all the squares together—it is easier to sew them in strips of 9, and then sew these lengths together.

CHART
The numbers on the chart represent the square pattern, while the letters represent the color. The same color is never repeated in any row of nine squares, nor in any square set of nine squares. It is impossible to get the patterns to do this at the same time, but as far as possible they have been positioned away from each other.

A3	C1	D6	H7	I8	E2	F7	B5	G7
F9	E3	I5	G2	B7	A4	H8	D1	C6
G1	B8	H3	D4	F2	C9	I2	A7	E5
D2	I4	G6	E8	H9	F5	A6	C3	B1
E1	H2	C4	A9	D5	B6	G5	F8	I7
B9	F6	A8	C7	G4	I9	D3	E4	H5
H4	D9	F1	B3	E6	G8	C5	I1	A2
C8	G3	B2	I3	A1	D7	E9	H6	F3
I6	A5	E7	F4	C2	H1	B4	G9	D8

Lace Cushion

This pretty lacy cushion cover by Laura Long is knitted in one long piece, and then the ends are folded over to make the back of the cover. The cushion inside will show through the lacy holes, so choose one with a cover to match or to contrast prettily with the yarn. The ribbon on the reverse looks great if it matches the cushion inside!

Materials

Yarn

Luxury Soft Cotton by Sirdar, 1¾oz/50g ball, each
approx 103yd/95m (100% unmercerized cotton)
4 balls in Bermuda Blue 664

Needles and extras

Pair US 10 (6.00 mm) needles
Yarn needle
6 buttons
28 in. (70 cm) ribbon cut in half
16 × 16 in. (40 × 40 cm) pillow form with a
matching or contrasting color cover

Gauge

19 sts and 28 rows to 4 in. (10 cm) over
stockinette stitch, on US 10 (6.00 mm) needles.
If necessary, change needle size to obtain this
gauge.

Sizes and Measurements

Actual measurements: finished cushion
16 × 16 in. (40 × 40 cm)

Cushion

Cast on 74 sts.
Work 4 rows reverse St st.
Work 83 rows in St st.

First part of front section:
Row 1 (WS): P4, [yo, p2tog, p1] 11 times, *p1, p2tog, yo; rep from * to last 4 sts, p4.
Row 2: Knit.
Row 3: P2 *p2tog, yo, p1, yo, p2tog, p25, p2tog, yo, p1, yo, p2tog; rep from * to last 2 sts, p2.
Row 4: Knit.
Row 5: P3, p2tog, yo, p28, p2tog, yo, p4, yo, p2tog, p28, yo, p2tog, p3.
Row 6: Knit.
Row 7: Purl.
Row 8: Knit.
Row 9: Purl.
Row 10: K3, k2tog, yo, k28, k2tog, yo, k4, yo, k2tog, k28, yo, k2tog, k3.
Row 11: Purl.
Row 12: K2 *k2tog, yo, k1, yo, k2tog, k25, k2tog, yo, k1, yo, k2tog, rep from * to last 2 sts, k2.
Row 13: Purl.

Row 14: K4, yo, k2tog, k28, yo, k2tog, k2, k2tog, yo, k28, k2tog, yo, k4.

Row 15: Purl.

Row 16: Knit.

Row 17: Purl.

Row 18: Knit.

First set of lace squares:

Row 19: P4, yo, p2tog, p4, [yo, p2tog, p1] 7 times, p3, yo, p2tog, p2, p2tog, yo, p4, *p2tog, yo, p1; rep from * to last 9 sts, p3, p2tog, yo, p4.

Row 20: Knit.

Row 21: P2, p2tog, yo, p1, yo, p2tog, p1, p2tog, yo, p1, yo, p2tog, p13, [p2tog, yo, p1, yo, p2tog, p1, p2tog, yo, p1, yo, p2tog] twice, p13, p2tog, yo, p1, yo, p2tog, p1, p2tog, yo, p1, yo, p2tog, p2.

Row 22: Knit.

Row 23: P3, p2tog, yo, p4, p2tog, yo, p16, p2tog, yo, p4, p2tog, yo, p4, yo, p2tog, p4, yo, p2tog, p16, yo, p2tog, p4, yo, p2tog, p3.

Row 24: Knit.

Row 25: Purl.

Row 26: Knit.

Row 27: Purl.

Row 28: K3, k2tog, yo, k4, k2tog, yo, k16, k2tog, yo, k4, k2tog, yo, k4, yo, k2tog, k4, yo, k2tog, k16, yo, k2tog, k4, yo, k2tog, k3.

Row 29: Purl.

Row 30: K2, k2tog, yo, k1, yo, k2tog, k1, k2tog, yo, k1, yo, k2tog, k13, [k2tog, yo, k1, yo, k2tog, k1, k2tog, yo, k1, yo, k2tog] twice, k13, k2tog, yo, k1, yo, k2tog, k1, k2tog, yo, k1, yo, k2tog, k2.

Row 31: Purl.

Row 32: K4, yo, k2tog, k4, yo, k2tog, k16, yo, k2tog, k4, yo, k2tog, k2, k2tog, yo, k4, k2tog, yo, k16, k2tog, yo, k4, k2tog yo, k4.

Row 33: Purl.

Row 34: Knit.

Row 35: Purl.

Row 36: Knit.

Row 37: P4, yo, p2tog, p4, yo, p2tog, p16, yo, p2tog, p4, yo, p2tog, p2, p2tog, yo, p4, p2tog, yo, p16, p2tog, yo, p4, p2tog yo, p4.

Repeat rows 20 to 31 once more.

Row 50: K4, yo, k2tog, k4, [yo, k2tog, k1] 7 times, k3, yo, k2tog, k2, k2tog, yo, k4, *k2tog, yo, k1, rep from * to last 9 sts, k3, k2tog, yo, k4.

Work next section:

Row 51: Purl.

Row 52: Knit.

Row 53: Purl.

Row 54: Knit.

Row 55: P4, yo, p2tog, p28, yo, p2tog, p2, p2tog, yo, p28, p2tog, yo, p4.

Row 56: Knit.

Row 57: P2 * p2tog, yo, p1, yo, p2tog, p25, p2tog, yo, p1, yo, p2tog, rep from * to last 2 sts, p2.

Row 58: Knit.

Row 59: P3, p2tog, yo, p28, p2tog, yo, p4, yo, p2tog, p28, yo, p2tog, p3.

Row 60: Knit.

Row 61: Purl.

Row 62: Knit.

Row 63: Purl.

Work second set of lace squares:

Row 64: K3, k2tog, yo, k4 [k2tog, yo, k1] 7 times, k3, k2tog, yo, k4, yo, k2tog, k4, *yo, k2tog, k1 rep from * to last 8 sts, k3, yo, k2tog, k3.

Row 65: Purl.

Row 66: K2, k2tog, yo, k1, yo, k2tog, k1, k2tog, yo, k1, yo, k2tog, k13, [k2tog, yo, k1, yo, k2tog, k1, k2tog, yo, k1, yo, k2tog] twice, k13, k2tog, yo, k1, yo, k2tog, k1, k2tog, yo, k1, yo, k2tog, k2.

Row 67: Purl.

Row 68: K4, yo, k2tog, k4, yo, k2tog, k16, yo, k2tog, k4, yo, k2tog, k2, k2tog, yo, k4, k2tog, yo, k16, k2tog, yo, k4, k2tog yo, k4.

Row 69: Purl.

Row 70: Knit.

Row 71: Purl.

Row 72: Knit.

Row 73: P4, yo, p2tog, p4, yo, p2tog, p16, yo, p2tog, p4, yo, p2tog, p2, p2tog, yo, p4, p2tog, yo, p16, p2tog, yo, p4, p2tog yo, p4.

Row 74: Knit.

Row 75: P2, p2tog, yo, p1, yo, p2tog, p1, p2tog, yo, p1, yo, p2tog, p13, [p2tog, yo, p1, yo, p2tog, p1, p2tog, yo, p1, yo, p2tog] twice, p13, p2tog, yo, p1, yo, p2tog, p1, p2tog, yo, p1, yo, p2tog, p2.

Row 76: Knit.

Row 77: P3, p2tog, yo, p4, p2tog, yo, p16, p2tog, yo, p4, p2tog, yo, p4, yo, p2tog, p4, yo, p2tog, p16, yo, p2tog, p4, yo, p2tog, p3.

Row 78: Knit.

Row 79: Purl.

Row 80: Knit.

Row 81: Purl.

Row 82: K3, k2tog, yo, k4, k2tog, yo, k16, k2tog, yo, k4, k2tog, yo, k4, yo, k2tog, k4, yo, k2tog, k16, yo, k2tog, k4, yo, k2tog, k3.

Repeat rows 65 to 76 once more.

Row 95: P3, p2tog, yo, p4 [p2tog, yo, p1] 7 times, p3, p2tog, yo, p4, yo, p2tog, p4, *yo, p2tog, p1; rep from * to last 8 sts, p3, yo, p2tog, p3.

Work next section:

Row 96: Knit.

Row 97: Purl.

Row 98: Knit.

Row 99: Purl.

Row 100: K3, k2tog, yo, k28, k2tog, yo, k4, yo, k2tog, k28, yo, k2tog, k3.

Row 101: Purl.

Row 102: K2 * k2tog, yo, k1, yo, k2tog, k25, k2tog, yo, k1, yo, k2tog, rep from * to last 2 sts, k2.

Row 103: Purl.

Row 104: K4, yo, k2tog, k28, yo, k2tog, k2, k2tog, yo, k28, k2tog, yo, k4.

Row 105: Purl.

Row 106: Knit.

Row 107: Purl.

Row 108: Knit.

Row 109: P4, yo, p2tog, p28, yo, p2tog, p2, p2tog, yo, p28, p2tog, yo, p4.

Row 110: Knit.

Row 111: P2 * p2tog, yo, p1, yo, p2tog, p25, p2tog, yo, k1, yo, p2tog, rep from * to last 2 sts, p2.

Row 112: Knit.

Row 113: P3, [p2tog, yo, p1] 11 times, p2, *p1, yo, p2tog, rep from * to last 3 sts, p3.

Work second half of back:

Work St st for 36 rows.

Next row (RS): K4, [yo, k2tog, k1] 11 times, *k1, k2tog, yo; repeat from * to last 4 sts, k4.

Work St st for 11 rows (ending with purl row).

Work 4 rows reverse St st.

Bind off.

Finishing

Position lace pattern at the front and fold the two back sections over, RS together. Sew neatly together along the side seams.

Thread the ribbon through the row of lace holes in the back and tie with a bow in the center.

Sew 6 buttons at equal distance along the edge of one side of the back opening, then make buttonhole loops on the other side to close opening.

Loopy Rug

A lovely touchable addition to any room, this handsome rug designed by Kate Buchanan is snuggly soft and very simple to make! The rug is made up of six garter stitch squares and six loop stitch squares, which are sewn together in a checkered pattern.

Materials

Yarn

Bigga by Sirdar, 3½oz/100g ball, each approx 149 yd/137 m (100% acrylic)

5 balls in Nutmeg (A)

6 balls in Kalahari (B)

Country Style by Sirdar, 3½oz/100g ball, each approx 346 yd/318 m (15% wool, 40% nylon, 45% acrylic)

Small amount in a toning color for making up

Needles and extras

1 pair US 15 (10 mm) needles

Darning needle

Gauge

7.5 sts and 15 rows to 4 in. (10 cm) over garter stitch, on US 15 (10 mm) needles.

6 sts and 10 rows to 4 in. (10 cm) over loop stitch, on US 15 (10 mm) needles. If necessary change needle size to obtain this gauge.

Sizes and Measurements

Actual measurements: finished rug 30 × 40 in. (75 × 100cm); **each square** 10in × 10in (25cm × 25cm)

Garter Square (make 6)

Using A, cast on 19 sts.

Continue to knit with garter stitch (knit every row) until the square measures 10 in. (25 cm)—this is approximately 38 rows in total.

Bind off.

Loop Square (Make 6)

Using B, cast on 15sts VERY LOOSELY.

Work loosely in loop stitch as follows:

Row 1: Do the following steps for every stitch on this row:

● Knit one stitch, keep the st on the right-hand needle, but do not slip the stitch off the left-hand needle.

● Bring the yarn forwards between the needles (as for purl) and hold a loop under the thumb, then take the yarn back between the needles.

● Knit into the same stitch and slip off.

● Pass the first stitch over the second.

Row 2: Knit.

These two rows make up the loop stitch pattern. The loops should be about ¾ in. (2 cm) tall.
Continue in patt until the square measures 10 in. (25 cm)—approximately 25 rows—ending on a knit row.
Bind off.

Finishing

Using slipstitch and DK yarn, sew the squares together alternately in a checkerboard pattern, using slipstitch or a flat seam (see page 62).
Fluff up the loops if necessary and snuggle up to enjoy your rug!

In the Loop

For best results, try to get the loops even and of the same length. This may take a bit of practice so try out a few sample squares first. You could make them into a matching cushion at the end!

Textured Cushion

This chunky textured cushion designed by Laura Long makes a stylish addition to any home. It is knitted in soft aran yarn so it is not only fast to make, but also great to snuggle up to on those long winter nights. The gauge is not really important for this project, but it is worth checking anyway if you want to cover a standard cushion.

Materials

Yarn
Supersoft Aran by Sirdar, 3½oz/100g ball, each
approx 257 yd/236 m (100% acrylic)
3 balls in Denim 870

Needles and extras
1 pair US 3 (3.25 mm) needles
1 pair US 7 (4.50 mm) needles
Yarn needle
3 toggle buttons
16 × 24 in. (40 × 60 cm) pillow form

Gauge
9 sts and 14 rows to 4 in. (10 cm) over stockinette
stitch, on US 3 (3.25 mm) needles. If necessary
change needle size to obtain this gauge.

Sizes and Measurements
Actual measurements: 16 × 24 in. (40 × 60 cm)

Cushion
Using US 3 (3.25 mm) needles, cast on 47 sts.
Work 2 rows of reverse St st.
Row 7: *P2, k1; rep from * to last 2 sts, p2.
Row 8: *K2, p1; rep from * to last 2 sts, k2.
Repeat rows 7 and 8 ten times more.

Work textured pattern for front:

Row 1: Using US 3 (3.25 mm) needles, p2, *k into front, back, front, back of st, p2, k1, p2; rep from * to last 3 sts, k into front, back, front and back of st, p2.

Row 2: Change to US 7 (4.50 mm) needles, *K2, [k1 winding yarn round needle twice] four times, k2, p1; rep from * to last 8 sts, k2, [k1 winding yarn round needle twice] four times, k2.

Row 3: P2, *k4 dropping extra loops, p2, k1, p2; rep from * to last 6 sts, k4 dropping extra loops, p2.
Repeat rows 2 and 3.

Row 6: Change to US 3 (3.25 mm) needles, *K2, p4tog, k2, p1; rep from * to last 8 sts, k2, p4tog, k2.

Row 7: P2, * k1, p2, k into front and back of st, p2; rep from * to last 3 sts, k1, p2.

Row 8: Change to US 7 (4.50 mm) needles, *K2, p1, k2, [k1 winding yarn round needle twice] four times; rep from * to last 5 sts, k2, p1, k2.

Row 9: *P2, k1, p2, k4 dropping extra loops; rep from * to last 5 sts, p2, k1, p2.
Repeat rows 8 and 9.

Row 12: Using US 3 (3.25 mm) needles, *K2, p1, k2, p4tog; rep from * to last 5 sts, k2,p1, k2.

These 12 rows form textured pattern. Repeat rows 1–12 three times more.

Make other half of back:
Using US 3 (3.25 mm) needles, work in St st for 41 rows, ending with a k row.
Next row: Knit.
Next row: Purl.
Bind off.

Making up

Place the textured section RS down and fold over the two back pieces so the ribbed section overlaps the plain section. Stitch the side seams.

Sew the toggle buttons on the plain back section and make button loops at the edge of the ribbed back section to match.

Comfort Zone

This great cushion has been made rectangular so it is ideal to use on a bed—or to tuck along the arms of a comfy chair.

The yarn is quite chunky and the stitches are large, so although the textured pattern is not that open, the cushion beneath may show through a little. Choose a plain fabric cover in the same color as the yarn to prevent this from happening.

The toggle fastenings go well with the denim color of the yarn, but there is no reason why you should not choose another type of button if you wish.

The textured design forms loose bobbles on the front surface. Do not press the work when you have finished or these will be flattened out of shape. If you wash the cushion later, just pull it gently back into shape and leave to dry flat.

Babies & Children

Childrenswear should be colorful and spirited, and the projects in this chapter are designed specially for the wee set. A Baby Argyle Cardigan makes an ideal cover-up at the playground and the Grrrrr Tiger Scarf will keep your little one looking and feeling *grrrrr-reat* during winter months. Finally, the sumptuous Baby Afghan would make a delightful gift for any soon-to-be Mommy.

Baby Argyle Cardigan

Created by Kate Buchanan, this is the cutest little cardigan for that very special baby. A combination of colorwork and Swiss darning—which is sometimes known as duplicate stitch—gives a modern take on the classic Argyle diamond design.

Materials

Yarn

Snuggly DK by Sirdar, 1¾oz/50g ball, each approx 190 yd/175 m (55% nylon, 45% acrylic)

2 balls in Mauve 341 (A)

1 ball in Green 378 (B)

Small amount in Pretty Lemon 843 (C)

Needles and extras

1 pair US 6 (4 mm) circular needles

5 × yellow buttons approx. ⅝ in. (15 mm) diameter

4 stitch markers

Yarn needle

Gauge

24 sts and 31 rows to 4 in. (10 cm) over stocking stitch, on US 6 (4 mm) needles. If necessary change needle size to obtain this gauge.

Sizes and Measurements

To fit: 0-6 months (6-12 months)

Actual measurements: chest 20½ (24) in. [52 (60) cm]; **length** 25 (27½) in. [10 (11) cm]; **sleeve** 6 (6¼) in. [15 (15.5) cm]

Special technique—Swiss darning

Swiss darning is a type of embroidery stitch, which follows the knitted stitches of stockinette stitch to look as if the design has been knitted. Fasten the yarn on the WS of the work and bring it up to the RS at the base of a knitted stitch. Then take the needle through the top of the knitted stitch from right to left, and then back through to the WS through the base again. This has "duplicated" on stitch in a contrast color on top of the original stitch. Repeat on top of as many stitches as required to create the design.

The Circle Line

This is not a "knitting in the round" pattern, but since the whole of the body is worked in one piece, a circular needle makes the number of stitches more manageable! Although the design has three colors, any sts shown on the chart in color C are worked in A, as C is sewn over the top in Swiss darning later.

Body

Using B, cast on 48 (58) sts for neck edge.

Row 1: *K1, p1; rep from * to end.

Row 2: *P1, k1; rep from * to end.

Repeat row 1.

Repeat row 2, placing markers after 8, 15, 33, 40 (10, 18, 40, 48) sts.

Change to A.

Next row: *Knit to one st before marker, m1, k2, m1; rep from * 3 times, k to end.

Next row: Purl.

Repeat last 2 rows 19 (22) times more: 208 (242) sts.

First sleeve:

Knit to second marker, cast on 2 sts, turn.

Purl to first marker, cast on 2 sts, turn.

The sleeve is worked across these 51 (58) sts.

Working in St st, dec 1 st at beg and end of every fourth row, 8 times: 35 (42) sts.

Work 6 (8) rows St st.

Next row: *K1, p1; rep from * to last 1 (0) st, k1 (0).

Next row: K1 (0), *p1, k1: rep from * to end.

Rep these 2 rows 3 times more.

Bind off.

Second sleeve:

Rejoin yarn A at under arm of completed sleeve, pick up 4 sts along the 4 cast on sts and knit to last marker, cast on 2 sts, turn.

Purl to third marker, cast on 2 sts, turn.

Working in St st, dec 1 st at beg and end of every fourth row, 6 (7) times: 35 (42) sts.

Work 6 (8) rows.

Next row: *K1, p1; rep from * to last 1 (0) st, k1 (0).

Next row: K1 (0), *p1, k1: rep from * to end.

Rep these 2 rows 3 times more.

Bind off.

Rejoin A yarn at under arm of second sleeve, pick up 4 sts along the 4 cast on sts and k to end of row.

Next row: P25, place marker, p to last 10sts, place marker, p10.

Continuing to work in St st, place chart design by working to marker, then working across 15 sts of chart, working St st to second marker, working across 15 sts of chart again, work to end of row. Remember to work all sts shown in color C on chart in A instead, as color C is added later with Swiss darning. Continue to work all 24 rows of chart.

Work 3 (5) rows of St st in A only.

Change to B, work 1 row St st.

Next row: *K1, p1; rep from * to end of row.

Rep this row 3 times more.

Bind off.

Note: Work flat band on left side for girls and right side for boys.

Flat band:

With B and RS facing, pick up 53 (63) sts along front edge, picking up about 2 sts for every 3 rows.

Next row: *K1, p1; rep from * to last st, k1.

Rep 5 times more.

Bind off.

Buttonhole band:

With B and RS facing, pick up 53 (63) sts along front edge, picking up about 2 sts for every 3 rows.

Next row: *K1, p1; rep from * to last st, k1.

Repeat this row once.

Button row 1: K1, p1, k1, p0 (1) bind off 2sts, *work as set for 9 (11) sts, bind off 2sts, rep from * to last 4 (5) sts, k0 (1), p1, k1, p1, k1.

Button row 2: K1, p1; rep to bound off sts, turn, cast on 2sts, turn, *work as set for 9 (11) sts, turn, cast on 2sts, turn; rep from * to last 3 (4) sts, p0 (1), k1, p1, k1.

Next row: *K1, p1; rep from * to last st, k1.

Repeat this row once.

Bind off.

Finishing

Join sleeve seams.

Position buttons under buttonholes and sew onto flat button band.

Using C, thread a yarn needle and complete design using Swiss darning technique and following chart for position of stitches.

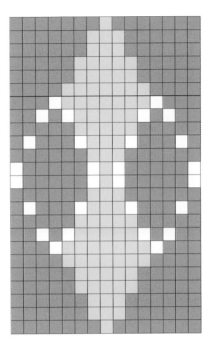

Mabel Cable Hat

*Kate Buchanan's snazzy child's hat is made using cozy yarn with
a touch of cashmere. The cable pattern gives the hat its unusual shape.
Use a scattering of odd buttons to finish it off with that unique touch!*

Materials

Yarn

RYC Cashsoft DK by Rowan, 1¾oz/50g ball, each
   approx 142 yd/130 m (57% extra fine merino
   wool, 33% microfiber, 10% cashmere)
1 ball in Madame 00511 (A)
1 ball in Lime 00509 (B)

Needles and extras

1 pair US 6 (4 mm) needles or a circular needle of
   this size
36 buttons in assorted shapes and sizes to match B
4 stitch markers
Cable needle
Sewing thread to match B
Yarn and sewing needles

Gauge

22 sts and 32 rows to 4 in. (10 cm) over stockinette
   stitch, on US 6 (4 mm) needles. If necessary
   change needle size to obtain this gauge.

Special Abbreviations

C4B = cable for back. Slip next 2 sts onto cable
   needle and leave at back of work, k2, then k2
   from cable needle.
C4F = cable for front. Slip next 2 sts onto cable
   needle and leave at front of work, k2, then k2
   from cable needle.
T4B = twist for front. Slip next 2 sts onto cable
   needle and leave at back of work, k2, then p2
   from cable needle.
T4F = twist for front. Slip next 2 sts onto cable
   needle and leave at front of work, p2, then k2
   from cable needle.

Hats Off

This hat is made in one wide flat strip so it might be
easier to knit it using a circular needle rather than
straight needles.

Even though there are funny things going on with the
cable pattern, always knit a knit stitch and purl a purl
stitch and you will be fine.

Sizes and Measurements

To fit: head circumference 18½ (20, 21) in. [46 (50, 53) cm]

Actual measurements: external width 9¼ (10, 10½) in. [23 (25, 26.5) cm]; length 7¼ (7¼, 7¾) in. (18 (18, 19) cm)

Hat

Using B, cast on 106 (116, 122) sts.

Knit into the back loop of every st.

Starting with a purl row on WS, work St st for 16 (16, 18) rows.

Next row (WS): Knit.

Starting with a knit row, work St st for 16 (16, 18) rows.

Change to A and work 2 rows of St st, placing markers after 4, 32, 56, 84 (5, 36, 62, 93, 6, 38, 66, 98) sts.

To place cable pattern, knit to first marker, work 18 sts of cable pattern as shown below, knit to next marker, repeat pattern. Continue for all 4 markers, finish by knitting to end of row. On WS, purl to 18 sts BEFORE each marker, work next row of cable pattern. Finish by purling to end of row. After a few rows, you will begin to see where the cable pattern is placed on the WS. Always knit the knit sts and purl the purl sts!

Work cable pattern:

Row 1 (RS: knit to markers): P3, k4, p4, k4, p3.

Row 2 (WS: purl to 18 before markers): K3, p4, k4, p4, k3.

Row 3: P3, C4F, p4, C4B, p3.

Row 4: K3, p4, k4, p4, k3.

Row 5: P3, k2, T4F, T4B, k2, p3.

Row 6: K3, p2, k2, p4, k2, p2, k3.

Row 7: P3, k2, p2, C4F, p2, k2, p3.

Row 8: K3, p2, k2, p4, k2, p2, k3.

Row 9: P3, k2, T4B, T4F, k2, p3.

Row 10: K3, p4, k4, p4, k3.

Repeat cable pattern from Row 3, three times more.

Next row (RS: knit to markers): P3, C4B, p4, C4F, p3.

Next row (RS): Purl, removing markers as you go.

Work 4 (4, 6) rows of St st.

Bind off.

Finishing

With wrong sides together, join side seam using mattress stitch. Fold flat so that the side seam is running up the center of one side of the hat—this side will become the back. Join the bound off edges together. Arrange buttons on the upper half of the headband. Sew in place. Fold the headband up inside the hat with the line of purl stitches on the fold line and wrong sides together. Lightly tack in place with yarn A.

> ### On Your Mark...
>
> When working with hanging stitch markers, always hang the marker in front for knit and at the back for purl to prevent the marker becoming caught up in the knitting!
>
> If you don't have custom stitch markers, a small length of contrast yarn threaded through the work and tied in a loose knot will work just as well.
>
> If you have to leave your knitting for more than a week, when you come back to it, unravel the last row and work from the one beneath. Stitches left too long on the needle can pull out of shape and this would show as a ridge in the final fabric.

Grrrrr Tiger Scarf

Knit this funky tiger-striped scarf designed by Kate Buchanan for your little Tigger!
The striking color combination gives a twist to the normal garter stitch scarf.
This project is very easy to knit and uses stranding, a technique in which you can
carry the yarn not being used across the back of the work.

Materials

Yarn
Matchmaker Merino DK by Jaeger, 1¾oz/50g ball,
    each approx 131 yd/120 m (100% merino wool)
1 ball in Pumpkin 898 (A)
1 ball in Bison 728 (B)

Needles and extras
1 pair US 7 (4.5 mm) needles

Gauge
22 sts and 40 rows to 4 in. (10 cm) over garter
    stitch, on US 7 (4.5mm) needles, although
    gauge is not important on this project.

Grand Strand
The contrast triangles are worked using stranding, a
technique where the yarn that is not being worked is
carried across three stitches—see page 47 for more
detail on this. It is important not to pull this strand tight
but also make sure it is not too loose if you want a really
neat finish!

Sizes and Measurements
Actual measurements: width 4 in. (10 cm);
length 38½ in. (98 cm) plus 3 in. (7 cm) fringe at
each end.

Scarf
Using A, cast on 22 sts.
Work 4 rows of garter st.
Join B onto A (do not cut yarn A).
Row 1: With B, k3, pick up A and k to end of row.
Row 2: With A, k19, yf, lay A over B, with B, yb, k3.
Row 3: With B, k6, pick up A and k to end of row.
Row 4: With A, k16, yf, lay A over B, with B, yb, k6.
Continue in this way until 15 sts have been worked in
B. Finish on a WS row.
Row 11: With B, k12, pick up A underneath B and k
to end of row.
Row 12: With A, k10, yf, lay A over B, with B, yb,
k12.
Row 13: With B, k9, pick up A underneath B and k
to end of row.
Row 14: With A, k13, yf, lay A over B, with B, yb, k9.
Continue in this way finishing on a WS row working
last 3 sts in B. Cut B.
Row 19: With A, k19, join B and k3.
Row 20: With B, k3, yf, lay B over A, with A, yb, k19.
Row 21: With A, k16, pick up B and k6.
Row 22: With B, k6, yf, lay B over A, with A, yb, k16.
Continue in this way until 15 sts have been worked in
B. Finish on a WS row.
Row 29: With A, k10, pick up B and k12.
Row 30: With B, k12, yf, lay B over A, with A, yb,
k10.
Row 31: With A, k13, pick up B and k9.
Row 32: With B, k9, yf, lay B over A, with A, yb, k13.
Continue in this way finishing on a WS row working
the first 3 sts in B. Cut B.
These 36 rows form the pattern of a B triangle
pointing into the center from each side. Repeat this
pattern until 21 triangles have been worked in total.

With A, work 4 rows of garter st.
Bind off.

Finishing
Weave ends into appropriate color so they don't
show. If necessary, back the wrong side of the scarf
with suitable soft lining fabric.

Make fringes:
Cut 40 × 8 in. (20 cm) strands of each color. Make a
tassel from 2 strands of each color. Attach 10 tassels
to each end of the scarf. Trim the ends of the fringe
so that it measures about 3 in. (7 cm).

For Kid's Sake
The strands of yarn on the back of this scarf are very
short, so will not pose a hazard for a small child and
the design is almost reversible. However, if you are
worried that the strands might catch and pull, you can
either line the back of the scarf with a length of fabric,
or go over the loops with spare yarn and a darning
needle to catch them in.

The jolly colors of this scarf were specially chosen to
look like a tiger's stripes, but you can make your scarf
in any color you like—tigers sometimes come in black
and white too!

Sunflower Hat

Bring some extra sunshine into life with this bright sunflower hat designed by Louise Butt! The 3-D petals on the top make your little one look really cute—and will certainly make a child stand out in a crowd. The hat is designed in two sizes and is quite simple to make.

Materials

Yarn

Cotton DK by Debbie Bliss, 1¾oz/50g ball, each
   approx 91 yd/84 m (100% cotton)
2 balls in green 13033 (A)
2 balls in yellow 13035 (B)
2 balls in brown 13032 (C)

Needles and extras

1 pair of US 5 (3.75 mm) needles
1 pair of US 6 (4 mm) needles

Gauge

20 sts and 28 rows to 4 in. (10 cm) over stocking
   stitch, on US 6 (4 mm) needles. If necessary
   change needle size to obtain this tension.

Sizes and Measurements

To fit: 1-2 (2-4) years.

Hat

Cast on 72 (86) sts using US 5 (3.75mm) needles and A.
Work 6 rows in 2 x 2 rib (K2, P2).

Next Row: Rib 6 (8), *m1, rib 6 (7), rep from * to last 0 (1) st, K0 (1): 83 (99) sts.

Change to US 6 (4 mm) needles.
Row 1: Purl.
Row 2: K6 (9), *m1, K7 (8), rep from * end: 94 (108) sts.
Row 3: Purl.
Row 4: K6 (9), * m1, K8 (9), rep from * to end: 105 (119) sts.
Row 5: Purl.
Row 6: K6 (9), * m1, K9 (10), rep from * end: 116 (130) sts.
Row 7: Purl.
Row 8: K8 (10) *m1, K9 (10), rep from * to end: 128 (142) sts.
Row 9: Purl.
Row 10: Knit.

Row 17: P5 with B, p6 with A, *p8 with B, p6 with A, rep from * to last 5 sts, p5 with B.

Row 18: K5 with B, k6 with A, *k8 with B, k6 with A, rep from * to last 5 sts, k5 with B.

Row 19: P6 with B, p4 with A, *p10 with B, p4 with A, rep from * to last 6 sts, p6 with B.

Row 20: K6, with B, k4 with A, *k10 with B, k4 with A, rep from * to last 6 sts, k6 with B.

Row 21: Purl in B.

Row 22: Knit in B.

Row 23: Purl in B.

Add petals:

Row 24: In B make first petal: K3, *p10, turn and working on just these 10 sts:

K10, turn,

P2tog, p6, p2tog tbl, turn,

K8, turn,

P2tog, p4, p2tog tbl, turn,

K6, turn,

P2tog, p2. p2tog tbl, turn,

K4, turn,

P2tog, p2tog tbl, turn,

K2, turn.

Cast off last 2 sts pwise*.

Make petals on main part of hat:

Row 11: Join in B, *p2 with B, p12 with A; rep from * to last 2 sts, p2 with B.

Row 12: *K2 with B, k12 with A, rep from * to last 2 sts, k2 with B.

Row 13: P3 with B, p10 with A, *p4 with B, p10 with A, rep from * to last 3 sts, p3 with B.

Row 14: K3 with B, k10 with A, *k4 with B, k10 with A, rep from * to last 3 sts, k3 with B.

Row 15: P4 with B, p8 with A, *p6 with B, p8 with A rep from * to last 4 sts, p4 with B.

Row 16: K4 with B, k8 with A, *k6 with B, p8 with A, rep from * to last 4 sts, k4 with B.

Next petals:

**Rejoin yarn, k4, rep from * to *; then rep from ** to last 3 sts, rejoin yarn, k3.

Row 25: P3, *pick up and p10 sts across top of petal, p4; rep from * to last 3 sts, p3: 128 (142) sts.

Row 26: K7 (10), *k2tog, k9; rep from * to end: 117 (120) sts.

Row 27 and every alt row: Purl.

Row 28: K7 (0) *K2tog, k8; rep from * to end: 106 (108) sts.

Row 30: K7 (0)*K2tog, k7; rep from * to end: 95 (96) sts.

Row 32: K7 (0)*K2tog, k6; rep from * to end: 84 sts.

Row 34: K7 (0) *K2tog, k5; rep from * to end: 73 (72) sts.

Row 36: K1 (0) *K2tog, k4; rep from * to end: 61 (60) sts.

Fasten off A and B.

Make flower center:

Join in C.

Row 38: K1 (0) *K2tog, k3; rep from * to end: 49 (48) sts.

Row 40: K1 (0) *K2tog, k2; rep from * to end: 37 (36) sts.

Row 42: K1 (0) *K2tog, k1; rep from * to end: 25 (24) sts.

Row 44: K1 (0), K2tog to end.

Now cut a long end of yarn, thread it through the 13 (12) stitches on your needle and pull tightly. Secure the yarn end.

Finishing

Sew up seam and weave in the ends.

Color codes

The colors for this hat have been chosen to match those of a sunflower, but you could substitute white for the yellow yarn B and yellow for the brown yarn C and make a Daisy Hat instead.

If you need to work out how much yarn you will need for an area of color within a pattern, check the number of stitches in this color and then wrap the end of the yarn around the needle the same number of times. Unravel and measure the yarn, adding a little extra for working with, then multiply the length by the number of rows. This tells you the length of yarn needed for that area of color. For number of balls of yarn needed, you can check this measurement against the ball band, which will tell you the average length of yarn in each ball.

It does take a bit of practice to get the tension even when switching between two colors of yarn. Be careful not to work too loosely as you change yarn, as this will lead to the knitting being more open as you change color. Also try not to over compensate and pull the yarn too tight as you swap colors.

Baby Blanket

Keep baby snug, tucked under this wonderful double seed-stitched baby blanket. The Aran-weight yarn will be warm and cozy, while the simple pattern creates a breathable layer. The colors chosen here by Louise Butt are suitable for either a boy or a girl, but you can make yours in whichever shade you like.

Materials

Yarn

Supersoft Aran by Sirdar, 3½oz/100g ball, each approx 257 yd/236 m (100% acrylic)
3 balls in Pretty Blue 844 (A)
3 balls in Pretty Lemon 843 (B)
1 ball in Pretty Green 845 (C)

Needles and extras

1 pair of US 8 (5 mm) needles

Gauge

18 sts and 24 rows to 4 in. (10 cm) over double moss stitch, on US 8 (5 mm) needles. If necessary change needle size to obtain this gauge.

Sizes and Measurements

Actual measurements: 31½ × 47¼ in. (80 × 120 cm)

Squares (Make 3 squares in each of yarn A and B)
Cast on 72 sts.
Row 1: [K2, p2] repeat to end of row.
Row 2: As row 1.
Row 3: [P2, k2] repeat to end of row.
Row 4: As row 3.
These 4 rows form double moss stitch pattern. Rep these 4 rows until square measures 16 in. (40cm). Bind off.

Long seam cover (Make 2)
Cast on 6 sts with C.
Knit every row until knitting measures 47¼ in. (120 cm).

Short seam cover (Make 2)
Cast on 6 sts with C.
Knit every row until knitting measures 31½ in. (80 cm)

Finishing

Darn in all ends. Join squares to create a checkerboard pattern, with all stitches facing the same direction.
Using backstitch and a matching yarn, sew the two shorter seam covers so they sit directly over the seam.
Using backstitch and a matching yarn, sew on the long seam cover so that it sits directly over the seam.

Stitch Library

Now that you've mastered the basic techniques, your
knitting has reached an entirely new level where you can
create your own designs or even alter existing patterns. This
chapter provides you with some beginner and advanced
stitches so instead of creating a stockinette-stitched scarf,
you can design something with an all-over or lace-and-
eyelet pattern. You are only limited by your own creativity.

All-Over Patterns

Moss stitch
Multiple of 2 sts + 1
Drape: good
Skill: easy

Row 1: K1, *p1, k1; rep from * to end.
Rep this row.

Little Ladders
Multiple of 6 sts + 4
Drape: good
Skill: easy

Row 1 (RS): Knit.
Row 2: P4, *k2, p4; rep from * to end.
Row 3: Knit.
Row 4: P1, k2, *p4, k2; rep from * to last st, p1.
Rep these 4 rows.

Seed Stitch Rib
Multiple of 4 sts + 3
Drape: good
Skill: easy

Row 1 (RS): P1, k1, *p3, k1; rep from * to last st, p1.
Row 2: K3, *p1, k3; rep from * to end.
Rep these 2 rows.

Diamond Brocade
Multiple of 8 sts + 1
Drape: good
Skill: easy

Row 1 (RS): K4, *p1, k7; rep from * to last 5 sts, p1, k4.
Row 2: P3, *k1, p1, k1, p5; rep from * to last 6 sts, k1, p1, k1, p3.
Row 3: K2, *p1, k3; rep from * to last 3 sts, p1, k2.
Row 4: P1, *k1, p5, k1, p1; rep from * to end.
Row 5: *P1, k7; rep from * to last st, p1.
Row 6: As Row 4.
Row 7: As Row 3.
Row 8: As Row 2.
Rep these 8 rows.

Basketweave Stitch
Multiple of 8 sts + 3
Drape: good
Skill: easy

Row 1 (RS): Knit.
Row 2: K4, p3, *k5, p3; rep from * to last 4 sts, k4.
Row 3: P4, k3, *p5, k3; rep from * to last 4 sts, p4.
Row 4: As Row 2.
Row 5: Knit.
Row 6: P3, *k5, p3; rep from * to end.
Row 7: K3, *p5, k3; rep from * to end.
Row 8: As Row 6.
Rep these 8 rows.

Spiral Pattern
Multiple of 7 sts
Drape: good
Skill: easy

Row 1 (RS): P2, k4, *p3, k4; rep from * to last st, p1.
Row 2: K1, p3, *k4, p3; rep from * to last 3 sts, k3.
Row 3: P1, k1, p2, *k2, p2, k1, p2; rep from * to last 3 sts, k2, p1.
Row 4: K1, p1, k2, p2, *k2, p1, k2, p2; rep from * to last st, k1.
Row 5: P1, k3, *p4, k3; rep from * to last 3 sts, p3.
Row 6: K2, p4, *k3, p4; rep from * to last st, k1.
Row 7: P1, k5, *p2, k5; rep from * to last st, p1.
Row 8: K1, p5, *k2, p5; rep from * to last st, k1.
Rep these 8 rows.

Little Checks
Multiple of 6 sts +3
Drape: good
Skill: easy

Row 1 and every alt row: Knit.
Row 2: Knit.
Rows 4 and 6: P3, *k3, p3; rep from * to end.
Rows 8 and 10: Knit.
Rows 12 and 14: K3, *p3, k3; rep from * to end.
Row 16: Knit
Rep these 16 rows.

Looe Eddystone
Multiple of 11 sts
Drape: good
Skill: easy

Row 1 and every alt row (RS): Knit.
Row 2: P2, k7, *p4, k7; rep from * to last 2 sts, p2.
Row 4: P3, k5, *p6, k5; rep from * to last 3 sts, p3.
Row 6: P4, k3, *p8, k3; rep from * to last 4 sts, p4.
Rows 8 and 10: P5, k1, *p10, k1; rep from * to last 5 sts, p5.
Work 4 rows in St st.
Rep these 14 rows.

Eyelet and lace patterns

Little Flowers
Multiple of 6 sts + 3
Drape: good
Skill: intermediate

Row 1 (RS): Knit.
Row 2 and every alt row: Purl.
Row 3: Knit.
Row 5: *K4, yf, sl 1, k1, psso; rep from * to last 3 sts, k3.
Row 7: K2, k2tog, yf, k1, yf, sl 1, k1, psso, *k1, k2tog, yf, k1, yf, sl 1, k1, psso; rep from * to last 2 sts, k2.
Rows 9 and 11: Knit.
Row 13: K1, yf, sl 1, k1, psso, *k4, yf, sl 1, k1, psso; rep from * to end.
Row 15: K2, yf, sl 1, k1, psso, k1, k2tog, yf, *k1, yf, sl 1, k1, psso, k1, k2tog, yf; rep from * to last 2 sts, k2.
Row 16: Purl.
Rep these 16 rows.

Staggered Eyelets
Multiple of 4 sts + 3
Drape: good
Skill: intermediate

Work 2 rows in St st, starting with a knit row.
Row 3 (RS): *K2, k2tog, yf; rep from * to last 3 sts, k3.
Work 3 rows in St st, starting with a purl row.
Row 7: *K2tog, yf, k2; rep from * to last 3 sts, k2tog, yf, k1.
Row 8: Purl.
Rep these 8 rows.

Cell Stitch
Multiple of 4 sts + 3
Drape: excellent
Skill: intermediate

Row 1 (RS): K2, *yf, sl 1, k2tog, psso, yf, k1; rep from * to last st, k1.
Row 2: Purl.
Row 3: K1, k2tog, yf, k1, *yf, sl 1, k2tog, psso, yf, k1; rep from * to last 3 sts, yf, sl 1, k1, psso, k1.
Row 4: Purl.
Rep these 4 rows.

Lacy Rib
Multiple of 3 sts + 1
Drape: excellent
Skill: intermediate

Row 1 (RS): K1, *k2tog, yo, p1; rep from * to last 3 sts, k2tog, yf, k1.
Row 2: P3, *k1, p2; rep from * to last 4 sts, k1, p3.
Row 3: K1, yf, sl 1, k1, psso, *p1, sl 1, yo, k1, psso; rep from * to last st, k1.
Row 4: As second row.
Rep these 4 rows.

Lacy Diamonds

Multiple of 6 sts + 1
Drape: excellent
Skill: intermediate

Row 1 (RS): *K1, k2tog, yf, k1, yf, k2tog tbl; rep from * to last st, k1.

Row 2 and every alt row: Purl.

Row 3: K2tog, *yf, k3, yf, [sl 1] twice, k1, p2sso; rep from * to last 5 sts, yf, k3, yf, k2tog tbl.

Row 5: *K1, yf, k2tog tbl, k1, k2tog, yf; rep from * to last st, k1.

Row 7: K2, *yf, [sl 1] twice, k1, p2sso, yf, k3; rep from * to last 5 sts, yf, [sl 1] twice, k1, p2sso, yf, k2.

Row 8: Purl.
Rep these 8 rows.

Fishtail Lace

Multiple of 8 sts + 1
Drape: excellent
Skill: intermediate

Row 1 (RS): K1, *yf, k2, sl 1, k2tog, psso, k2, yf, k1; rep from * to end.

Row 2: Purl.

Row 3: K2, *yf, k1, sl 1, k2tog, psso, k1, yf, k3; rep from * last 7 sts, yf, k1, sl 1, k2tog, psso, k1, yf, k2.

Row 4: Purl.

Row 5: K3, *yf, sl 1, k2tog, psso, yf, k5; rep from * to last 6 sts, yf, sl 1, k2tog, psso, yf, k3.

Row 6: Purl.
Rep these 6 rows.

Fir Cone

Multiple of 10 sts + 1
Drape: excellent
Skill: intermediate

Row 1 (WS): Purl.

Row 2: K1, *yf, k3, sl 1, k2tog, psso, k3, yf, k1; rep from * to end.
Rep the last 2 rows three times more.

Row 9: Purl.

Row 10: K2tog, *k3, yf, k1, yf, k3, sl 1, k2tog, psso; rep from * to last 9 sts, k3, yf, k1, yf, k3, sl 1, k1, psso.
Rep the last 2 rows three times more.
Rep these 16 rows.

Garter Stitch Eyelet Chevron

Multiple of 9 sts + 1
Drape: excellent
Skill: intermediate

Row 1 (RS): K1, *yf, sl 1, k1, psso, k4, k2tog, yf, k1; rep from * to end.

Row 2: P2, *k6, p3; rep from * to last 8 sts, k6, p2.

Row 3: K2, *yf, sl 1, k1, psso, k2, k2tog, yf, k3; rep from * to last 8 sts, yf, sl 1, k1, psso, k2, k2tog, yf, k2.

Row 4: P3, *k4, p5; rep from * to last 7 sts, k4, p3.

Row 5: K3, *yf, sl 1, k1, psso, k2tog, yf, k5; rep from * to last 7 sts, yf, sl 1, k1, psso, k2tog, yf, k3.

Row 6: P4, *k2, p7; rep from * to last 6 sts, k2, p4.
Rep these 6 rows.

Cable and Twisted Stitch patterns

Simple Lattice
Multiple of 12 sts + 14
Drape: good
Skill: intermediate

Row 1 (RS): K4, C3B, C3F, *k6, C3B, C3F; rep from * to last 4 sts, k4.
Row 2 and every alt row: Purl.
Row 3: K3, C3B, k2, C3F, *k4, C3B, k2, C3F; rep from * to last 3 sts, k3.
Row 5: *K2, C3B, k4, C3F; rep from * to last 2 sts, k2.
Row 7: K1, *C3B, k6, C3F; rep from * to last st, k1.
Row 9: K11, *C4B, k8; rep from * to last 3 sts, k3.
Row 11: K1, *C3F, k6, C3B; rep from * to last st, k1.
Row 13: *K2, C3F, k4, C3B; rep from * to last 2 sts, k2.
Row 15: K3, C3F, k2, C3B, *k4, C3F, k2, C3B; rep from * to last 3 sts, k3.
Row 17: K4, C3F, C3B, *k6, C3F, C3B; rep from * to last 4 sts, k4.
Row 19: K5, C4B, *k8, C4B; rep from * to last 5 sts, k5.
Row 20: Purl.
Rep these 20 rows.

Raised Circles
Multiple of 7 sts + 1
Drape: good
Skill: intermediate

Row 1 (RS): P3, k2, *p5, k2; rep from * to last 3 sts, p3.
Row 2: K3, p2, *k5, p2; rep from * to last 3 sts, k3.
Row 3: P2, C2B, C2F, *p3, C2B, C2F; rep from * to last 2 sts, p2.
Row 4: K2, p4, *k3, p4; rep from * to last 2 sts, k2.
Row 5: P1, *C2B, k2, C2F, p1; rep from * to end.
Row 6: K1, *p6, k1; rep from * to end.
Row 7: P1, *k6, p1; rep from * to end.
Row 8: As row 6.
Row 9: P1, *T2F, k2, T2B, p1; rep from * to end.
Row 10: As row 4.
Row 11: P2, T2F, T2B, p3, T2F, T2B; rep from * to last 2 sts, p2.
Row 12: As row 2.
Rep these 12 rows.

Squares & Twists
Multiple of 10 sts + 4
Drape: good
Skill: intermediate

Row 1 (WS): P4, *k2,
p2, k2, p4; rep from *
to end.
Row 2: K4, *p2, C2B,
p2, k4; rep from * to
end.
Rep the last 2 rows
once more.
Row 5: K1, p2, *k2, p4,
k2, p2; rep from * to
last st, k1.
Row 6: P1, C2B, *p2,
k4, p2, C2B; rep from
* to last st, p1.
Rep the last 2 rows
once more.
Rep these 8 rows.

Cable & Rib
Multiple of 9 sts + 5
Drape: fair
Skill: intermediate

Row 1 (RS): P2, KB1,
p2, *k4, p2, KB1, p2;
rep from * to end.
Row 2: K2, PB1, k2,
*p4, k2, PB1, k2; rep
from * to end.
Row 3: P2, KB1, p2,
*C4B, p2, KB1, p2;
rep from * to end.
Row 4: As row 2.
Rep these 4 rows.

Honeycomb
Multiple of 8 sts + 2
Drape: fair
Skill: intermediate

Row 1 (RS): Knit.
Row 2: Purl.
Row 3: K1, *C4B, C4F;
rep from * to last st,
k1.
Row 4: Purl.
Rows 5 and 6: As rows
1 and 2.
Row 7: K1, *C4F, C4B;
rep from * to last st,
k1.
Row 8: Purl.
Rep these 8 rows.

Double Cable
Worked over 12 sts on a
background of reverse
St st.
Skill: intermediate

Row 1 (RS): K12.
Row 2: P12.
Row 3: C6B, C6F.
Row 4: P12.
Rows 5 and 6: As rows
1 and 2.
Rep these 6 rows.

Ribs and Edgings

Cable & Garter
Multiple of 10 sts + 8
Drape: good
Skill: intermediate

Row 1 (RS): Knit.
Row 2: P7, *k4, p6; rep from * to last st, p1.
Rep the last two rows twice more.
Row 7: K1, C6F, *k4, C6F; rep from * to last st, k1.
Row 8: As row 2.
Row 9: Knit.
Rep the last two rows twice more.
Row 14: P2, k4, *p6, k4; rep from * to last 2 sts, p2.
Row 15: Knit.
Rep the last two rows twice more, then row 14 again.
Row 19: K6, *C6B, k4; rep from * to last 2 sts, k2.
Row 20: As row 14.
Row 21: Knit.
Rep the last two rows twice more, then row 14 again.
Rep these 24 rows.

Feather Rib
Multiple of 5 sts + 2
Drape: fair
Skill: intermediate

Row 1 (RS): P2, *yo, k2tog tbl, k1, p2; rep from * to end.
Row 2: K2, *yf, k2tog tbl, p1, k2; rep from * to end.
Rep these 2 rows.

Fisherman's Rib
Multiple of 2 (or 3)
  sts + 1
Drape: fair
Skill: intermediate

Note: Each set of
  instructions gives the
  same appearance but
  a different 'feel'. For
  example, C is a firmer
  fabric than A.

Method A
Multiple of 2 sts + 1

Foundation row: Knit.
Row 1 (RS): Sl 1, *K1B,
  p1; rep from * to end.
Row 2: Sl 1, *p1, K1B;
  rep from * to last 2
  sts, p1, k1.
Rep the last 2 rows only.

Method B
Multiple of 2 sts + 1

Foundation row: Knit.
Row 1 (RS): Sl 1, *K1B,
  k1; rep from * to end.
Row 2: Sl 1, *k1, K1B;
  rep from * to last 2
  sts, k2.
Rep the last 2 rows only.

Method C
Multiple of 3 sts + 1

Row 1 (RS): Sl 1,
  *k2tog, yo, sl 1
  purlwise; rep from *
  to last 3 sts, k2tog,
  k1.
Row 2: Sl 1, *yo, sl 1
  purlwise, k2tog (the
  yo and sl 1 of previous
  row); rep from * to
  last 2 sts, yo, sl 1
  purlwise, k1.
Rep the last 2 rows.

Picot Point Bind Off
Multiple (in edge to be
  bound off) of 3 sts +
  2
Drape: as main fabric
Skill: easy

Bind off 2 sts, *slip
  remaining st on right
  needle onto left
  needle, cast on 2 sts,
  bind off 4 sts; rep
  from * to end and
  fasten off remaining
  stitch.

165

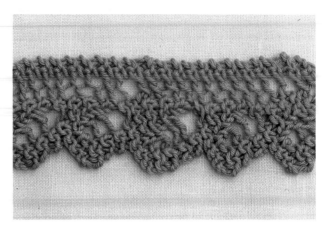

Point Edging

Drape: good

Skill: intermediate

Note: each point is worked separately.

Cast on 2 sts.

Row 1: Knit.

Row 2: Yo (to make a stitch), k2.

Row 3: Yo, k3.

Row 4: Yo, k4.

Row 5: Yo, k5.

Row 6: Yo, k6.

Row 7: Yo, k7.

Row 8: Yo, k8.

Row 9: Yo, k9.

Row 10: Yo, k10.

Row 11: Yo, k11.

Row 12: Yo, k12.

Rows 1–12 form one point. Break yarn and leave finished point on needle. On the same needle cast on 2 sts and work second point.

Continue in this way until there are as many points as required. Do not break yarn after completing the last one, but turn and knit across all points on needle.

Work 9 rows in Garter st.

To finish, sew back ends.

Butterfly Edging

Worked over 8 sts

Drape: fair

Skill: intermediate

Cast on 8 sts.

Row 1 (RS): Sl 1, k2, yo, k2tog, [yo] twice (to make 2 sts), k2tog, k1. (9 sts)

Row 2: K3, p1, k2, yo, k2tog, k1.

Row 3: Sl 1, k2, yo, k2tog, k1, [yo] twice, k2tog, k1. (10 sts)

Row 4: K3, p1, k3, yo, k2tog, k1.

Row 5: Sl 1, k2, yo, k2tog, k2, [yo] twice, k2tog, k1. (11 sts)

Row 4: K3, p1, k4, yo, k2tog, k1.

Row 7: Sl 1, k2, yo, k2tog, k6.

Row 8: Bind off 3 sts (first on right needle), k4, yo, k2tog, k1. (8sts)

Rep these 8 rows.

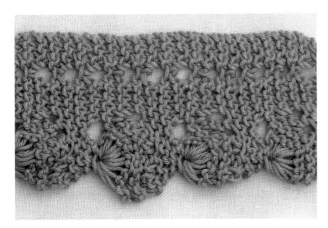

Puffball Cluster Edging
Worked over 13 sts
Drape: good
Skill: experienced

Special abbreviation
YF2—yarn forward twice to make 2 sts.
Cast on 13 sts.

Row 1 (RS): K2, k2tog, YF2, k2tog, k7.
Row 2: K9, p1, k3.
Rows 3 and 4: Knit.
Row 5: K2, k2tog, YF2, k2tog, k2, [YF2, k1] 3 times, YF2, k2. (21 sts)
Row 6: K3, [p1, k2] 3 times, p1, k4, p1, k3.
Rows 7 and 8: Knit.
Row 9: K2, k2tog, YF2, k2tog, k15.
Row 10: Knit 12 sts wrapping yarn twice round needle for each st, YF2, k5, p1, k3. (23 sts)
Row 11: K10, [p1, k1] into next st, slip next 12 sts to right needle dropping extra loops; return sts to left needle then k12tog. (13 sts)
Row 12: Knit.
Rep these 12 rows.

Fancy Leaf Edging
Worked over 17 sts
Drape: good
Skill: intermediate
Cast on 17 sts.

Row 1 (RS): K3, yo, p2tog, yo, p2tog, yo, KB1, k2tog, p1, yb, sl 1, k1, psso, KB1, yo, k3.
Row 2: K3, p3, k1, p3, k2, yo, p2tog, yo, p2tog, k1.
Rep the last 2 rows once more.
Row 5: K3, yo, p2tog, yo, p2tog, yo, KB1, yo, k2tog, p1, yb, sl 1, k1, psso, yo, k4. (18 sts)
Row 6: K4, p2, k1, p4, k2, yo, p2tog, yo, p2tog, k1.
Row 7: K3, yo, p2tog, yo, p2tog, yo, KB1, k1, KB1, yo, sl 1, k2tog, psso, yo, k5. (19 sts)
Row 8: K5, p7, k2, yo, p2tog, yo, p2tog, k1.
Row 9: K3, yo, p2tog, yo, p2tog, yo, KB1, k3, KB1, yo, k7. (21 sts)
Row 10: Bind off 4 sts (1 st remains on right needle), k2, p7, k2, yo, p2tog, yo, p2tog, k1. (17 sts)
Rep these 10 rows.

Aftercare

After spending so much time, care and attention creating your hand-knitted item, you will want to care for it properly so that it will last for years to come. Hand-knitted items will not stand repeat washing as well as machine-made ones, but as long as you follow some basic rules they should still be fine. First read the information on the recommended cleaning for the yarn, which you will find on the ball band. It is a good idea to keep a length of the yarn you have used and one ball band—the yarn will be useful if you have to carry out repairs later, while the ball band will be a reference for cleaning instructions in the future.

Storage

Store knitted items folded on a shelf, or in a closed drawer, if possible. Do not hang on hangers, as they will stretch out of shape. If an item will be stored for some time, make sure it is clean and dry and pack in a large plastic bag. Use a proper repellent in the storage space to keep moths away—natural materials such as cedar wood can be effective, or use chemical strips or mothballs.

Hand-washing

Use lukewarm water and a mild detergent specially formulated for knitted items. Keep the item under water and squeeze it gently all over to clean—do not lift it out of the water, which may stretch it, or rub, which may damage the surface of the yarn or pull stitches. Let the water out, squeezing gently to remove as much of the water trapped in the yarn as possible. Rinse several times in lukewarm water, then again squeeze gently to remove as much water as possible. Do not wring, just press and squeeze. Some yarns my be suitable for tumble-drying—check the ball band. If not, lay the item out on a clean, colorfast towel and pull it gently into shape. Leave it to dry away from direct heat. If necessary, press when dry following the instructions on page 59.

Machine Washing

Some yarns are suitable for machine washing—check the ball band. Choose a program that matches the symbols on the ball band and stick to the recommended water temperature. It can be a good idea to wash jumpers inside a colorfast bag such as a pillowcase, as this will keep them confined and less likely to stretch. Remove the item from the machine as soon as the cycle finishes and leave it to dry as described above.

Dry cleaning

If the ball band says the yarn can be dry cleaned, make sure the dry cleaner is aware of the symbols given as these indicate which chemicals should be used. Do not dry clean items that can be washed—it will not prolong their life and the chemicals may be harmful to the yarn. Ask the dry cleaner not to hang the item on a hanger, or to press it.

Abbreviations

approx	approximately		**PB**	place bead (see page 54)
alt	alternate		**PB1**	purl into back of next stitch
beg	beginning		**PU**	pick up and knit
C4B	Cable 4 Back (see page 49)		**PM**	place marker
C4F	Cable 4 Front (see page 50)		**psso**	pass slipped stitch over
T3B	Twist 3 Back (see page 51)		**p2tog**	purl two stitches together
T3F	Twist 3 Front (see page 52)		**pw**	purlwise
ch	chain		**rem**	remaining
cm	centimeter		**rep**	repeat
cont	continue		**RS**	right side(s)
dec	decrease		**sl**	slip
foll	following		**st(s)**	stitch(es)
in.	inch(es)		**St st**	stockinette stitch
inc	increase		**tbl**	through back of loop(s)
k	knit		**tog**	together
KB1	knit into back of next stitch		**WS**	wrong side(s)
k2tog	knit two stitches together		**yd.**	yard
kw	knitwise		**wyib**	with yarn in back
m	meters		**wyif**	with yarn in front
mm	millimeters		**yb**	yarn behind between two needles to back
oz	ounce		**yf**	yarn forward between two needles to front
p	purl		**yo**	yarn over

Glossary of Knitting Terms

Aran – a traditional style of patterned textured knitting that originated from the Aran Islands, which are off the coast of Ireland.

Argyle – a geometric pattern with large diamond shapes in two or three colors overlaid with a pattern of diagonal lines in a contrasting color.

Backstitch – a stitch used to join two pieces of fabric together, with even, small stitches forming a straight, continuous line on one side and longer, overlapping stitches on the reverse, see page 62.

Ball band – the paper band round a ball or hank of yarn when it is purchased, which gives the brand name, ply and fiber content of the yarn, the shade and dye lot, recommended gauge, needle sizes and washing instructions.

Binding off – the term used in the US for securing the stitches permanently when a piece of knitting is finished, see page 37.

Blanket Stitch – a type of embroidery stitch that is normally used to finish off a raw edge.

Blocking – the pinning out of each piece of knitting to the correct shape and dimensions before pressing, see page 58.

Bobble – a group of stitches worked several times, producing a raised bobble on the right side of the fabric, see page 53.

Cable – a method of moving a group of stitches across the fabric, or crossing one set of stitches over another, to make a pattern like a rope.

Cable needles – short, double-pointed needles used when moving groups of stitches in cable or twisted stitch patterns

Casting off – the term used in the UK for binding off.

Casting on – the term used for making the first row of stitches. There are a number of different methods, see pages 22-25.

Charts – a visual representation of a pattern, showing the exact placement of colors or stitches on a grid. They are usually used in conjunction with written pattern instructions, see also page 18.

Continental method – a way of knitting in which the right needle is held in the right hand like a knife, and the left over the top. The working yarn is controlled with the left hand. It is faster than the English method, but it is harder to get an even, consistent stitch.

Damp finishing – a method of damping the finished piece of knitting so it can be flattened and pulled into shape without steam pressing. It is used for synthetic yarns and when the knitting is highly textured, see page 59.

Decrease – the term for reducing the number of stitches on the needle. There are several methods, see pages 33, 40–1.

Decorative decreasing – another term for fully-fashioning, see page 40–1.

Dye lot – a number given to each dye batch of yarn in the same shade.

English method – a way of knitting in which the right needle is held in the right hand like a pen, and the left over the top. The working yarn is controlled with the right hand. It is slower than the Continental method, but produces a more consistent, even stitch.

Fair Isle – a pattern created in many different colors in stockinette stitch. Each row is worked in two or more colors, although there may be many more colors used in the full design. The color yarn not being used at any one time is carried across the back of the fabric, producing a double thickness. This type of knitting originated in the Shetland Isles, off Scotland. See page 46.

Flat seam – a method of overcasting edges that produces a completely flat seam, see page 62.

Fully-fashioned – a term used to describe a garment in which the decreases are worked one or two stitches in from the edge, creating a decorative effect. This technique is most often used on raglan sleeves.

Garter stitch – term for the most basic knit pattern, in which every row is either knit or purl to produce a knitted fabric that is exactly the same on each side. It is also sometimes called plain knitting and is often used for bands or edgings.

Gauge – the US term for the way in which stitch size is measured. Correct gauge will give you the same size and shape item as specified in the pattern.

Increase – term used for a method of shaping a piece of knitted fabric by adding stitches as you knit. See pages 34–5 and 38.

Intarsia – the name given to multi-colored knitting in which separate balls of yarn are used for each area of color so, unlike Fair Isle, the yarn not in use is not carried across the back of the fabric but joined in as required. There may be any number of colors used in any given row. See page 44.

Knit stitch – the most basic stitch and usually the first that is learned, see pages 26–7.

Lace knitting – a decorative fabric created by increasing and decreasing stitches to form open areas in different patterns. It can be included in a pattern as an all-over design or in selected areas, bands or panels.

Mattress stitch – a stitch used for joining pieces of knitted fabric that creates an invisible seam, see page 60–1.

Overcasting – the US term for sewing over the edges of the knitted fabric to create a flat seam.

Oversewing – the UK term for overcasting.

Pattern repeat – an area of pattern made up of a set number of stitches that is repeated several times across a row.

Pilling – the term for little bobbles of fiber that sometimes appear on the surface of knitted fabric when it has been worn or rubbed. The bobbles can be removed with a special machine and will grow less over time.

Ply – the term for the strands of fiber that make up a yarn, but also used to distinguish the thickness of yarns.

Pressing – the method used to flatten pieces of knitted fabric before they are sewn together. Pressing not only gives a professional finish, but also helps the garment to hold its shape, see page 59.

Purl stitch – the second basic stitch in knitting, after knit stitch. The purl stitch is slightly more difficult to master, see page 28. When used in conjunction with knit stitch a whole range of very different patterns can be made.

Reverse stockinette stitch – the reverse side of a piece of stockinette stitch fabric.

Rib – a knitted pattern in which alternate kit and purl stitches are worked to create an elastic fabric. It is often used as the edging on hem and cuffs. Single rib is one stitch of knit and purl worked alternately, double rib is two stitches of each worked alternately. See page 48.

Right side – the side of the fabric that will be seen on the outside when the finished garment is worn.

Row counter – a small cylindrical device with a dial used to record the number of rows.

Shaping – the term used to describe making slopes to left or right by increasing and decreasing the number of stitches on the needle.

Slip knot – a loop created at the start of casting on, see page 21.

Slip stitch – a method of joining one fabric on top of another.

Slipping stitch – a stitch that is passed from one needle to another without being worked.

Split ring marker – little clips that can be attached to knitting to mark the beginning of a round in circular knitting, or for marking points in a stitch pattern.

Stockinette stitch – the US term for the most common knitted fabric, which is created by working alternate knit and purl rows, see page 28.

Stocking stitch – the UK term for stockinette stitch.

Stranding – a method of carrying the yarn that is not in use loosely across the back of the work, as in Fair Isle. See page 47.

Stitch holder – a holder like a large safety pin used to hold stitches that will be worked on later.

Swatch – a knitted sample piece of the overall fabric, usually made to check the stitch gauge.

Tension – the UK term for gauge.

Texture knitting – creating a texture on the surface of the knitting by combining knit and purl stitches.

Unraveling – undoing a piece of knitted fabric stitch by stitch, or row by row, which can be done with the knitting on or off the needles, see page 68–9.

Weaving – a method of catching the yarn not in use across the back of the work, when it is being carried more than 3 or 4 stitches. See page 47.

Wrong side – the side of the fabric that will be on the inside, and so not normally seen, when the finished garment is worn.

Suppliers

USA

Berroco, Inc.
Elmdale Rd.
Uxbridge, MA 01569
Tel: (508) 278-2527

Caron International
P.O. Box 222
Washington, NC 27889
www.caron.com

Coats & Clark
Consumer Services
P.O. Box 12229
Greeneville, SC 29612-0224
Tel: (800) 648-1479
www.coatsandclark.com

Colinette
Distributed by Unique Kolours
28 N. Bacton Hill Road
Malvern, PA 19355
Tel: (610) 644-4885
www.uniquekolours.com

Debbie Bliss, Katia, Sirdar
Distributed by Knitting Fever, Inc.
315 Bayview Avenue
Amityville, NY 11701
Tel: (515) 546-3600
www.knittingfever.com

Lion Brand Yarn Co.
34 West 15th St.
New York, NY 10011
Tel: (212) 243-8995

Patons
320 Livingstone Avenue South
Listowel, ONT N4W 3H3
Tel: (888) 368-8401
www.patonsyarns.com

Red Heart® Yarns
Two Lakepointe Plaza
4135 So. Stream Blvd.
Charlotte, NC 28217
www.coatsandclark.com

Rowan, Jaeger
Distirbuted by
Westminster Fibers. Inc.
3 Northern Boulevard, Suite 3
Amherst, NH 03031
www.westminsterfibers.com

Twilleys
Distributed by S.R Ketzer Ltd.
50 Trowers Road
Woodbridge, ONT L4L 7K6
Tel: (905) 856-3447
www.twilleys.co.uk

Canada

Colinette, Debbie Bliss, Jaeger, Katia, Rowan, Sirdar
Distributed by Diamond Yarns
9697 St Laurent
Montreal, QC H3 2N1
Tel: (514) 388-6188
www.diamondyarn.com

Patons
320 Livingstone Avenue South
Listowel
Ontario
N4W 3H3
Tel: (888) 368-8401
www.patonsyarns.com

Twilleys
Distributed by S.R Ketzer Ltd.
50 Trowers Road
Woodbridge, ONT L4L 7K6
Tel: (905) 856-3447
www.twilleys.co.uk

Index

Acknowledgments

The Designers

Kate Buchanan is the founder of the Westender Stitch 'n' Bitch knitting group in Ealing and was a finalist in the UK National Knitting Award 2005 with the design "Biastripe." She teaches hand knitting at London's Chelsea College of Art and Design and has designed several projects for *Simply Knitting* magazine. In 2005 she launched a range of knitting kits, GiftedKnits, which includes a Learn To Knit kit with CD. Kate designed the following projects in this book: Stripy Joe, Heirloom Wrap, Reversible Fair Isle Carryall, Pod Pocket Cozy, Loopee Rug, Baby Argyle Cardigan, Mable Cable Hat and Grrrrr Tiger Scarf.

Louise Butt started knitting and crocheting at the age of seven and began designing both knitting and crocheting garments for sale in her mother's yarn shop in her teens. After University she worked for a magazine publisher, while still knitting and crocheting in her spare time. Since January 2005 she has been Operations Editor on a UK magazine, *Simply Knitting*, and has designed many projects for publication in the magazine. Louise designed the following projects in this book: Drop-Stitch Cardigan, Cable Shrug, Cable-Tasseled Scarf, Foxy Cushion, Suduko Blanket, Sunflower Hat and Baby Blanket

Laura Long studied textiles (specializing in Knitwear) at London's Central St. Martin's School of Art, where she became interested in traditional Irish crafts such as lace, crochet, Aran knitting, and knotwork. After graduating with 1st class honors she was awarded a prestigious Textprint prize to exhibit at Indigo, Paris, followed by exhibitions at both London and Paris fashion weeks. She then worked in Ireland with the fashion designer John Rocha and is now involved in various knitwear design projects, including designing hand knitted garments and accessories for the Rowan seasonal magazines and designing and making garments and accessories for fashion houses. Laura designed the following projects in this book: Whimsical Winter Warmers, Textured Hat & Scarf, Lace Cushion and Textured Cushion

Sîan Luyken is an experienced hand-knitter who learned from her grandmother before she started school. She has designed garments for UK magazines such as *Simply Knitting* and *Magknits* and she is co-organizer of the London knitting group Angelknits. Sîan designed the following projects in this book: Cap-Sleeve Tunic, Seaweed Wrap, Ladder-Stitch Neckwarmer and Blue Note Hat & Scarf.